If I
Should Die
Before
I Live

Other books by the author:

Deeper Into John's Gospel

*New Directions from
the Ten Commandments*

When the Wood Is Green

If I
Should Die
Before
I Live

*With Study Guide
for Personal Reflection
or Group Interaction*

Arthur Fay Sueltz

WORD BOOKS
PUBLISHER
WACO, TEXAS

IF I SHOULD DIE BEFORE I LIVE

All Scripture quotations, unless otherwise noted, are from *The New English Bible* © The Delegates of the Oxford University Press and The Syndics of the Cambridge University Press, 1961, 1970. Reprinted by permission.

The quotation marked KJV is from the King James Version of the Bible.

Grateful acknowledgement is made for permission to quote the following:

Mind Song, "Minnie Remembers," by Donna Swanson, © 1978, Upper Room, Nashville, Tennessee.

MARC newsletter, "On Leaving Your Oldest Daughter," by Edward R. Dayton Copyright © September, 1973 by World Vision International.

ISBN 0-8499-0090-5
Library of Congress catalog card number: 78-65800
Printed in the United States of America

To Millie
in love and gratitude for
sharing this pilgrimage with me.

Contents

Foreword

Over one hundred years ago Charles Finney, lawyer turned evangelist and the founder of Oberlin College, drew great crowds wherever he spoke. Many traveled hundreds of miles on horseback or in wagons to hear him. One listener who had made such a trip on a number of occasions was asked by the press for the reason. "Mr. Finney talks about the things other men preach about," was the reply.

Art Sueltz, in the tradition of Charles Finney, does not preach. He talks about God and life. His book is based on the life of King David, one of my favorite heroes of the faith. Using David as a model, he examines the many ingredients of present day life: marriage, loneliness, success, illness, revenge, forgiveness, enemies, friends, depression, dreams, jobs, middle age, death, lust, joy, failure, boredom, tiredness and anger. This is a book about every person's journey of life in the light of God's love.

The author writes poignantly and personally, sharing the serendipity of "ah-ha" moments. His chapters are like giant ink blots in which each of us can find his own essence and direction. Art Sueltz has the gift of writing with authority without being authoritative. He is no old, emeritus sage passing on wisdom from a safe position of age or virtue. His authority comes from his identification with the reader.

Here is a book that is both timely and timeless, eternal and contemporary. The writing is psychologically sound without sounding psychological. It is theologically profound, without sounding theological. Like many of the people who have mastered their fields, whether in medicine, education, psychology or theology, Art does not have to hide behind professional jargon. He writes about life and life problems.

I would like to think that there are many communicators of the good news like Art. But my hope does not match my experience. Each generation has all too few who can shed light on the contemporary scene with such helpful simplicity and sincerity. I would be surprised if anyone could read this book without experiencing a change in attitude, outlook or behavior.

Bruce Larson

Preface

To a lot of us who came of age in the fifties and sixties, growing up meant getting through school, getting a job, getting married and having children. How we longed for a mortgage of our own complete with installment payments. What a thrill the first year we made enough money to pay income tax!

So we pushed our youth in front of us. We made it from carefree childhood to careworn middle-age in one breathtaking leap. And what did we find when we got there? Many of us have position, money, authority, and experience—and an inner turmoil so chaotic we can hardly get our hands on it.

What is a mature Christian person supposed to be? What is he or she supposed to do? Before we can get answers we must ask the right questions. In his closing remarks to the Princeton Seminary class of 1962, President James I. McCord told of Gertrude Stein who, on her deathbed, turned to her friend Alice Toklas and asked, "Alice, what is the answer?" Alice looked at her sadly and said, "Gertrude, I'm afraid we don't know." After a long pause Miss Stein said, "Well, then, what is the question?" The question always determines the answer. And understanding how to live is quite different from knowing how to make a living. I want to understand life in its primary dimensions.

Suppose I have committed my life to Christ. How do I develop spiritual maturity from that point of beginning? What if I should die before I live? That is a primary question. And I have discovered in the Bible "a man after God's own heart" through whose experience God gives me new insight into the basic issues of life.

1 ~ *Summertime*

Suddenly one summer the shadow of a really terrifying specter fell on me. It was the specter of a haunting dream like emptiness of life when a kind of dark prehistoric chaos broods over all our bright talk and activity.

One afternoon soon after that experience I stood behind a mother and several grown children in New York's Kennedy Airport. I thought I recognized them. I overheard them talking about a television review in the morning paper. And then I remembered. I'd seen them the night before on the Dick Cavett Show—the Louds of the television documentary, *An American Family*.

Painful things happened to the Loud family during the filming of that series. Lance, the oldest son, slid down into that strange subculture of homosexuality. Bill and Pat, the parents, got divorced after twenty years of marriage. But so many people can match painful family situations with any braggart.

Novelist Ann Riophe said, "If there is such a thing as negative culture or culture minus, the Louds have it. The blaring sound of rock is the high point of creativity in the family. They make a large fuss over clothes, but they're bought not made. There's no religion, no threatening Jehovah, no merciful Mary, no myths of Jupiter, no avenging sensibility, no moral right or wrong, no sense of judgment good or bad weighing over the family. In strict traditionalist societies, everyone knows the rules, the punishments for breaking them, what can or cannot be done. I think the Louds have escaped the small town mores of earlier America. They have been educated and led into a large vacuum, and like the rest of us are passed without the structures of work and religion that used to shape our days. We have so much freedom we are now culturally Neanderthal."

Freedom is one thing; chaos is another. Freedom means life; chaos death. Dark vacant empty chaos—that's the specter that threatens my life, spiritual and otherwise.

Unfortunately most people eventually turn thirty. To distrust everyone over thirty means that eventually I'll have to distrust myself.

In Franz Kafka's novel entitled *Trial*, Joseph wakes up on the morning of his thirtieth birthday and finds himself under arrest for an unnamed crime. He tries desperately to find out who has accused him and what he's accused of. But he dies on the eve of his thirty-first birthday without ever finding out. So Kafka keeps probing for meaning in a world which has lost faith in God and, along with that, faith in any certainty. Kafka's characters live in a world of frightening chaos and silence where people grope and ask questions but find no answers. And he suggests that the search often begins at age thirty. Until then a person drifts along at a very superficial level. Then one morning he wakes up to find himself in midstream facing disturbing mysteries in life.

Before this experience, Joseph took time for granted.

Only other people died. But now with the addition of a few years he begins to wonder what life means. Does life offer anything more than eating, drinking and trying to squeeze as much pleasure out of it as we can? And somehow a dark specter of chaos threatens to blot out the summer sun and to wreck lives, dash hopes and twist careers.

That specter haunts public as well as private life. I remember during the summer of 1973 sitting mesmerized before the television watching Senator Sam Ervin's special Senate committee investigating Watergate. And as I watched I sensed the same fearful specter haunting the hearing room. It didn't matter where one's sympathy lay. The story revealed wrecked lives, dashed hopes, and a growing confusion and betrayal haunting real people in high places. As Sir Thomas More, that man for all seasons, once said, "When men surrender their private conscience to achieve public ends they lead people on a short road to chaos."

And yet even my conscience working at its best may contribute to the uneasiness that boils up within me. Dr. William M. Jones in an article, *The White Man's Intolerable Burden*, suggests that we look at an ordinary boy born in the 1930s. As an eight-year-old he joked about beggars who came to the back door during the Depression. He attended First Church with his family and joined in the usual sexual experimentation of his age and class. He never thought twice about any of this, other than fervent hope that the police would never catch him or if they did that his father would bail him out. In short, he was a standard brand American Boy who read the magazine by the same name.

Then during World War II his family got ahead.

Following the war he went to college and received an engineering degree and went to work for IBM. But about ten years ago he took a job at State University. At the same time he began to read *Saturday Review of Literature* and similiar magazines rather than the old trade journals.

All at once a vague feeling of dissatisfaction began to shake the foundations of his life. He couldn't put his finger on it. But he found it in the people he ate lunch with. And he found it in the people he played golf with and in the corporations in which he did consulting work.

A lot of things buried for years began to surface. But instead of facing and admitting the guilt that came with a lot of senseless acts in his past, he took an opposite defensive approach. To shore up his emotional balance he suppressed his guilt and became "enlightened" or in the popular jargon "conscientized." He had a consciousness-raising experience.

Unfortunately his raised consciousness subtly placed on him a burden he hadn't expected—corporate guilt. All at once he felt it his duty to spread guilt around so everyone could have a little.

Instead of concentrating on the small circle of life over which he had some control, he saw the rotting inner city, the starving Biafricans, industrial pollution and said, "We are guilty!" At first he felt relieved. Instead of one guilt, one man, now everybody had a piece of the action. And of course along with others with raised consciences who saw this guilt, he now looked down on the other middle-class blockheads who wouldn't admit it. Instead of feeling guilty he now felt "righteous."

And yet somehow by taking on all the sins of his

unenlightened ancestors he made it impossible for himself
to ever get out from under any of it.

When I feel threatened by chaotic powers loose in the
world I want to hear from someone who has stared them
down. Such people speak to me in the Bible. They tell
me they discovered the Spirit of a living God brooding
over the chaotic forces in the world and in themselves and
calling them to order. In this Book I discover a lot of
people who began to get hold of life.

I don't know at what age Jesus began to think deeply
about life. I do read in the Gospels that something profound happened to him at about age thirty—something
that changed the history of the world, something that
drove him out into the desert for forty days to look life's
mysteries square in the face. In such moments a person
sees things that cannot be seen and yet are there. And
such a sight profoundly affects how he understands the
world and his place in it. Christ saw dangerous chaotic
events filled with the promises of God.

Yes, I may face events that threaten my life with chaos,
but they need not take the heart out of me. Intelligent
fear often proves to be the best way to conquer powerful
evil. Getting my priorities straight helps me fear the right
thing at the right time. What drives us to make better
schools if it isn't the fear of ignorance. Fear of disease
plunges us into medical research.

Other generations have faced disheartening chaotic
powers. A few years ago I saw the movie *The Last Ten
Days of Hitler*. I remembered how not so long ago Hitler
seemed on top of the world. He certainly thought he was.
He thought so during the 1936 Olympics. He thought so

during the blitzkrieg of Western Europe. In fact he had textbooks rewritten in Germany to teach the children things like: "The teaching of mercy and love for one's neighbor is foreign to the German race. The Sermon on the Mount is, according to Nordic sentiment, an ethic for cowards and idiots." But where is Hitler today?

Terrible things may yet happen to me, to my country, to my world. But I can't read history without feeling in my bones that people who create such chaos do not have the final word. And because I see that pattern repeating itself over and over it helps me straighten out my priorities. The powers of chaos do not have the last word; God does.

I've heard social scientists say that you can't change people. They admit you can teach a person speed reading or maybe belly dancing. But when it comes to the basic values a person holds, sociologists tend to feel that you can't teach an old dog new tricks.

I hear Jesus saying a man can experience a basic change in the way he sees life, the way he feels it, in the way he lives it. I hear him asking me to have faith in people not only as they are, but as by God's grace they may become. And he asks me to believe in myself not only as I am but as I may become.

That stance brings me to a whole new place of faith— faith in myself and faith in my society. Whatever else God may be he is just. He holds the powers of chaos accountable.

As Norman Cousins wrote, "If we read the signs correctly a new mood of confidence in the basic institutions and historical values of a nation is coming into being. People seem to sense that a vast cleansing process is at

work. The nation's moral climate is being restored,
. . . and the result is a vast regenerative experience. A
new sense of self-confidence is in the making. Till now
we have been like the man who had a deep itch and didn't
know where to scratch."

2 *It All Depends On Your Point of View*

Early Sunday morning I fished the *L. A. Times* from under my car, took it inside and over coffee scanned the front page. Then I looked for the opinion section with the editorials. The paper feeds me facts and opinions, but my reaction to what I read depends on my point of view. My job, where I live, what I believe, my past history affects how I understand what I see.

A small boy and his sister, complete with ice cream cones, drifted away from their mother in a large department store. Pretty soon they made a game out of going up and down in the elevator. Suddenly the boy noticed his cone dripping so he wiped it against the back of a woman's mink stole. "Watch yourself, Jimmy," said his sister. "You're getting fur in your ice cream." It all depends on your point of view.

A research psychologist once put two pictures into a stereoscope. The left eye saw a bull fighter, the right eye a baseball player. Then he asked some Americans and some Mexicans to look through the instrument. The Mexicans saw only the bullfighter. The Americans saw only the baseball player.

My hopes for spiritual development depend upon a continuous renewal of my point of view. What I see does not depend on my eyes alone. Nor does it depend on the events in front of me. I look out at the world from behind my eyes. What I see depends on my assumptions, my hopes, my dreams, my inner vision. I do not necessarily react to the facts in front of me; I react to what I understand those facts to be. That perception becomes reality for me. It shapes my behavior, it conditions my mood.

Two men once drove through the night in the bush land of our Southwest. The driver who had lived there all his life had a friend from the East with him. As they drove through the night they took a cut through the hills. Suddenly the Easterner let out a yell and scrambled over the front seat to the back and hid his face in his hands. He had seen what looked to him like a huge boulder dropping down onto the road in front of them. The driver didn't flicker an eyelash. He drove on. He knew the boulder was just a tumbleweed.

Both men saw the same event. And both acted reasonably for what they saw. But one man went into a spasm while the other's blood pressure didn't budge an inch. Why? Because of each man's inner vision of how the world looked to him. One man had developed an inner point of view that could handle a tumbleweed at night; the other had not.

So I suspect all people make reasonable decisions. It's just that sometimes my point of view has not prepared me to take hold of what life offers. And even at best I see through a glass darkly—I know only in part.

If I can change my point of view I might see the same world but everything will look different. In life that can be the most important thing that happens to me. I can change jobs, move into a new neighborhood, leave the country completely and still remain much the same kind of person. But a basic shift in my angle of vision will change everything—my values, my priorities, and how I spend my time.

Throughout history many people have said they suddenly caught sight of a new vision and began to look at the world with new eyes, to understand it with new minds, to use their energies in new ways.

All of us live by our inner visions. Sometimes we get flashes of insight that come completely unannounced. I remember once facing a meeting of angry people. I remember suddenly being aware of the calm of loving things worth loving. I understood in that instant there's more to life than I now see in me or around me. Ever since then when I get into such a situation it helps to remember that night and how the world looked at that moment.

Those moments of awareness are not frequent. Often love turns to grudging duty. But the fact remains that I do have a choice. I don't have to be a grouch before my first cup of coffee in the morning. I have a choice. I choose what inner vision I will give myself to. I choose my point of view. I can choose a point of view that shouts orders and gets satisfaction from feeling depressed. But I don't have to see the world that way.

If we forget all the rest of the Old Testament most of us remember the story of David and Goliath—the little guy and the bully. We root for the underdog because we hope everybody will get a fair break in life. Not everyone gets that break, of course, but once in a while justice gets done.

The story of David and Goliath reads like a shoot-out at the O.K. Corral. Suddenly the huge shadow of Goliath falls across the valley. Pound for pound who could match him with his brass helmet, brass shield, brass leggings, brass everything? But with one shout from Goliath all Israel trembles.

At that moment, as in any good Western, the hero appears, unexpectedly—David—young, handsome, lean, and a crack shot—the first of the quick drawers.

King Saul offers David his armor. David tries it. But it doesn't fit. He sees he'll have to fight this giant his own way. David's point of view allows him to see opportunities in the situation no one else has seen. Everyone else fights with spears and swords and defends themselves with shields.

And suddenly behind the scenes I see the real lineup in that valley of decision, the same lineup I see behind the scenes in so many events of my own times. On one side are the fearful whose point of view allows them to say only, "We've never done it that way before." And on the other side are a few who see beyond all the dead weight of common sense. They somehow know circumstances don't defeat people. People's inner perceptions defeat them. Opportunities exist even in threatening events if we can just see them.

So I picture David going down into the valley to shoot

it out with Goliath—a massive, heavy man encased in tons of brass. He moves sluggishly at best and now all that armor slows him to a walk.

David, wearing only a light shepherd's tunic, runs down the hill to meet him in the valley. And suddenly I see it! I see what I think David saw. Given these circumstances, slow moving Goliath didn't have a chance! He was a sitting duck. Only David saw it. Fleet lightly clad David could run circles around Goliath. He saw it because of an inner point of view that allowed him to think beyond the usual ways of thinking and doing. He had a surprise for Goliath! It only took one shot.

It's a person's inner point of view that allows him to do the best things in the worst times. David had only a sling and five smooth stones. And I get to thinking how often I excuse my fears and failures complaining that I don't have enough talent to work with. Yet how often a man with just one talent in his hand will outperform another man loaded with ability. Why? Because of the way he sees the world and his willingness to trust what he sees and use what he has. None of us work under perfect conditions. And we often make our best contribution in the worst times. If we wait for good times, we'll wait forever.

To King Saul's credit he did not make David fight the battle his way. He did not insist that David wear his armor. He let the young man go. And I know how hard that is in life. I know the power and not-so-subtle temptation to impose the style of my generation on my sons.

Yet how many giants has my generation slain? As I check over the list I find militarism, secularism, racism, political corruption, and other massive evils before which

I often quail and accept defeat without so much as a fight.

Furthermore, it looks to me like David, from his inner point of view, saw God taking sides. He ran toward Goliath shouting, "You come to me with a sword and a spear and a dagger, but I come to you in the name of the Lord of hosts." He did not believe God stood on the sidelines of life aloof, nonpartisan, a spectator. David sensed that all human history gets made behind our backs. He felt God at work in the world steadily seeing that his purposes work out. And David believed that in those plans God had a place for him and great work for him to do.

Any person who goes to meet a giant facing him assuming that he has a loving God beside him will time and again outthink and outperform monstrous chaotic evils. Little people who look so weak you'd think the next strong wind would blow them away suddenly stand up to anything.

On the other hand, Mark writes in his Gospel how one Friday Jesus at about age thirty-three led a parade into Jerusalem. And when he got to the temple Mark says, "He looked around at everything." And suddenly I wonder how things looked to him. For just a minute I forget how things look to me. That phrase stops me in my tracks.

Somehow I feel myself standing in the crowd as he "looked around at everything," and I begin to wonder how it looked from his inner point of view. What kind of an impression do I make? What goes on in his mind as he sees me? And for a minute or two I forget the point of view of my friends, my wife, or even the gospel writer and try to think of Christ. How do things look to him?

What does he think of the ambivalence he must see in me? That mixture of faith and fear, loyalty and betrayal, love and selfishness. Under the skin of every Christian lives a deserter. Yes, I believe I follow a great Christ, but he's dangerous. How easy to love him in the abstract, how difficult in the concrete.

A man worked all morning one day laying a concrete driveway. Worn out, he went in for some lunch. As he sat down he happened to look out the window and see some neighborhood children coming along with sticks. They began to write their names and draw pictures and other things in the fresh cement. He bolted out of his chair and through the door chasing them off with great roaring curses. When he came back into the house, panting and flush, his wife said, "John, I thought you loved children."

"I do love children in the abstract," he said, "but not in the concrete!"

Well, in the abstract I want hungry people fed but when it comes to getting at the root causes of hunger, that's not so easy. There are difficult questions like: why do Kansas farmers receive less for their products and consumers have to pay more and people across the seas go hungry? What causes that kind of chaos?

In the abstract many people believe in the idea of Christian marriage—that a man and woman live together till death do them part. But when a grouchy difficult husband or wife faces someone across the breakfast table every morning that abstraction suddenly becomes very concrete. In that situation all kinds of things begin to go on in a person's head and he may find himself rejecting the abstraction altogether.

I think as Jesus looks at me he sees all that ambivalence. He knows how often I reject what he stands for because I feel caught in the trap of my own conflcts, my own desires, my own security, my own fears and commitments.

And suddenly I see him coming right in to the middle of all my ambivalence. "And the Lord laid on him the iniquity of us all." He knows the evil that comes as a tragic result of my human ambivalence. But he also sees hope in the love with which I reach out to get hold of his hand. And as his eyes fall on me I sense not simply judgment, I sense healing and the grace of God.

And that point of view helps me see myself as someone God thinks highly of and calls by name. I think that's the greatest gift in the world—the gift of my self-esteem. When my existence makes God happy, who am I to feel miserable about myself? So in this day when songs have no tunes, when we often go through motions without meaning, I can live by an inner vision of God's spirit in my heart and in the hearts of other people in the streets of my community and the remote corners of the earth. It's the same old world. But now everything begins to look different.

3 *Conflict*

What chaos a little human conflict can kick up! Charlie Brown says, "No conflict's too big to run away from," but I've tried. Yet one glance at the cross tells me conflict lies somehow at the heart of the Christian faith, and I find the creative use of conflict essential to my spiritual development.

I live a life peppered with conflict. For instance, all of us carry different pictures in our heads of how people should dress, how they should act, what they should say, how they should spend their money. I usually come into conflict over such things with people I love the most. Perhaps it is because I care about those people that I feel so strongly about such matters.

A young man looks over at a young woman; she looks back. They both like what they see. A relationship begins to develop. Both show themselves to their best advantage; both avoid issues on which they might disagree. If an attitude or a mannerism vaguely displeases one of them he closes his eyes and hopes it will disappear.

These two people get married and suddenly they find themselves arguing. At first they try to smooth things

29

over. Chaos looms as a threat to their relationship. No one
ever told them that the argument isn't as important as the
way you fight and resolve or do not resolve the conflict.
So a union of soul mates soon dissolves into howling
chaos.

"But who can umpire a marital conflict? How can you
determine who is to blame?" asks Paul Tournier in his
book *The Healing of Persons*. Usually each person involved tells you his side of the story and wants you to
take sides. Very often both people in the conflict are
equally right and each has well-founded grievances.

When children come into the home conflict reaches out
to embrace them, too. On May 20, 1969, CBS presented
a news special entitled "Generations Apart." The com-
mentators realized that no one can generalize in a way to
include all young people, and no survey can claim complete accuracy. But their report revealed some fascinating
information. It showed that young people have a different
attitude toward money than older people. Eighty-three
percent of the college students believed America's wealth
is unjustly distributed. Ninety percent said big business
thinks too much about profits. These young people saw
their parents as products of the Depression who frantically
strive for more money long after the time of need has
passed.

The report revealed that adults and young people had
conflicting ideas about sex. Nine out of ten parents thought
of sex before marriage as a moral issue. But according to
CBS television, 46 percent of all young people and 64
percent of all college students do not see it as a moral
issue at all. These young people would substitute self-
fulfillment for legalism as a key to understanding sex.

And so for them sex with love but without marriage becomes a kind of protest against many conventional marriages which are loveless.

Now when conflict threatens to create chaos between husband and wife or parent and child we need to get beyond the apparent causes to the real ones. On the surface I hear conflicting ideas, opinions, ideals and tastes. But beneath these apparent causes often lie the real ones—fear, jealousy, self-centeredness, guilt, lack of honesty, and an unwillingness to accept differences.

Again God speaks through an experience in the life of David in the Old Testament. Early in his life David found himself in deadly conflict with the man he admired most —King Saul of Israel. The conflict was one that threatened to create chaos in the lives of both men and the entire country.

Saul, Israel's first king, was a complicated man. Born to lead, he stood head and shoulders above everybody else. The story of Saul and David's trouble starts out like this: suddenly in mid-career, depression began following Saul around like a black dog. No matter how happy he felt one day, the next he might feel terribly depressed. Sometimes he'd sit immobile for hours.

Depression often comes close on the heels of great success or great joy as though human nature cannot stand the strain success brings. A person gets the job, a promotion, makes the sale, and you'd think he would feel on top of the world for weeks. To the contrary, the next day he often pays for the excess of excitement with a fit of depression.

But depression has one great value—at a deep level it forces me to recognize something's missing, something has dropped out of my life. Depression always involves loss—loss of a friend, a job, or even one's value system. At the height of his power, King Saul suddenly felt something had dropped out of his life; he felt God's absence. With H. G. Wells he found God, "An ever absent help in time of trouble." To him it sometimes looked like God didn't know which side he was on.

One day when Saul needed help from God and tried to call it down nothing happened, "The Spirit of the Lord left him." That didn't make him weaker than anybody else. It just made him like everybody else. When he reached back for the power he needed he found nothing there. He began feeling insecure and threatened, so he withdrew and grew defensive and his moral judgments began going haywire.

Saul's friends asked David, a young folk singer and killer of giants, to come and try to raise the king's spirits. Everyone liked David. Not everyone can handle great popularity, but David could. Something about him cheered people up. As they listened to his songs a breath of hope stirred within them.

David also had the important talent of letting people love him. No one has such power to free people as a person who lets others love him. All of us must give our love to someone. Most of us give it within our families. But a lot of people for a variety of reasons have no one close at hand they can give their love to. When someone like David crosses the threshold of their lives, it's like a shower in the desert.

David entered Saul's tent. The king sat slumped on his chair, staring off into space. David began to sing a few popular ballads. Nothing happened. Saul didn't flicker an eyelash. Then all at once David began to sing about something he found all creation too small to convey. As he sang of the wind, the seas, the stars, the clouds, the animals and the trees, you could hear an echo of eternity. No wonder Jesus remembered and sang one of David's songs when he hung on the cross, "My God, why hast thou forsaken me." That song helped him through those dark hours.

As David sang Saul stirred. Slowly, cautiously, his eyes moved around the room, and his depression began to dissolve like fog before the sun. And Saul loved David for it.

Saul loved David, and David admired Saul. Then suddenly something happened—the king turned on David, the one who had done so much for him and meant so much to him, David the man he loved as he loved no one else. Why did Saul do this?

Suddenly Saul saw in David the kind of man he wanted to be and couldn't. Saul wanted the freedom, the charm, the wit, of David. He wanted to say things the way David said them. He tried and he couldn't. Everybody admired Saul, but everybody loved David. Saul desperately wanted people to love him like that.

God knows how I'm tempted to hate the person who did what I tried to do and couldn't. What conflict that creates between husbands and wives. They love each other and yet beneath the surface smoulders a hostility so great they sometimes feel like killing each other. Often they are two ambitious, intelligent people. But for years they play a subtle game of trying to outsmart each other. Each somehow feels threatened by the gifts or the success of the other. Instead of feeling happy about the success of the other they resent it and feel bitter.

But people can only live happily together when each wants the other to develop in his or her own way. Each must accept the other's right to his own feelings, his own thoughts, his own values and ideas. Each of us has a right to think and feel as we think and feel. When one of my wife's ideas bothers me I need to ask myself, "What is it in me that makes me feel this way toward her?" We can debate theories forever and never get together. When we get personal we give healing a chance.

Unfortunately I often feel that if I let my wife know how I really feel she might lose confidence in me, perhaps forever. But everything works just the opposite. The more I let her know the better our relationship becomes. I believe that if a man and woman want to stop living side by side like strangers they will have to pay that price. It frees people to combine their gifts instead of setting them against each other.

So David sang his songs that expressed how he felt toward his king, his world, and about himself. And that honesty helped Saul for a few hours. But then with little warning Saul slid down into fearful depression again. And David couldn't do much about it. Something evil caught and held both of them. And both of them saw it.

In a sense you can't blame either of them for it. Who can blame Saul for being taller than anyone else, for having those great gifts of leadership? Who can blame David for his charm and grace? Yet an irrational chaotic evil held them and plunged them into deadly conflict.

People still get caught in such conflicts—conflicts too deep for analysis, too subtle for our normal categories. In fact I talk to people suffering from a paralysis of analysis.

Saul felt powerless to pull himself out of the depression

into which his fears had pitched him. And David could do little to help no matter how hard he tried. In fact the harder he tried the worse it got. Sometimes it seems that resolution of such a conflict demands an act of God.

So many of us suffer from an insufficient religious experience. We need something far richer and more profound to sustain us. Cheerful pious chatter about all the possibilities life offers will not help for long. If it could, we ought to quit talking about Jesus Christ and dedicate our churches as shrines to success and happy feelings. But most thoughtful people yearn for something deeper than that.

So I look for David's greater Son, Jesus, the Christ in whom God acts to rescue us in those dark dangerous conflicts that defy analysis and go beyond our powers. How often he has lead me through conflict and brought me out on the other side a better, stronger person. Some conflicts I can't handle at all; they're beyond me. Someone stronger than I must take the field.

4 ⟩ *When You Need a Friend*

Every fall I see geese heading south flying along in V formation. Why do they fly that way? Why not in a cluster? Two aerodynamic engineers wondered the same thing, so they set up a wind tunnel experiment to find out. They quickly discovered that as each bird flaps his wings he creates an uplift for the bird that follows. By flying in V formation the whole flock adds 71 percent greater flying range than if each bird flew on his own. When a bird falls out of formation he suddenly feels the extra weight of trying to go it alone. How he'll scramble to get back into the uplifting wind current of the bird in front of him.

Watching those birds reminds me that I can't go it alone either. Of course I have to live my own life, but I do that best in relation to other lives. Sometimes I underrate that fact. But when I think about it, the greatest experiences I've had in life have come because of the invisible uplift given me by some true friends. And when I make a fool of myself they have the audacity to realize I haven't done a permanent job. When the rest of the world goes out, they come in. Without some real friends I could easily die before I live.

Some people give me a lift. Like the flame of one match igniting another, one person brings another alive. They enter the room and all kinds of new life starts stirring inside of me. I believe something like that happened between David and Jonathan. As long as Jonathan lived David felt the uplift of his life. Only after Jonathan died did David fall into tragic error. Two great friends. Jonathan made a difference in David's life. He brought out the best in him. And isn't that what we're here for? To bring out the best in each other. And the people who do that don't push me, or preach at me, or pressure me.

J. Wallace Hamilton in his book, *Serendipity*, tells of a young minister standing in a Cleveland railway station. He noticed a blind war veteran getting off the train with a heavy duffle bag. The minister went up and offered to carry the duffle bag. But the blind veteran shrugged him off and said he'd carry his own. "Well," said the minister, "can't I help you somehow? Can I take you somewhere?"

"Sure," said the veteran, "you can get me to the information desk." So the preacher took him firmly by the arm and started off. The blind veteran resisted and said, "Don't push me, pal. Don't try to possess me. All I need is a touch of your hand on my shoulder."

Who likes feeling pushed or preached at or possessed? Yet how many of us would give almost anything to have the uplifting touch of a friend's hand on our shoulder? Some of us in desperation try to buy friendship. We get tickets to a ballgame or a play and invite an interesting couple to go along. Unfortunately too often it doesn't work. They go along, but they never invite us back. Life gets lonely.

Of course not all friendships have the same value. A lot

of relationships get foisted on us. Two men sit down and have coffee together. They may not clash but they do not cooperate. They maintain a discreet personal distance. No real basis of trust exists, no real friendship.

Sexual relationships may also have such a personal distance and lack intimacy. A sexual relationship without the sharing of personal history, life goals and a commitment to faithfulness to each other's growth amounts to make-believe intimacy.

So some friendships can hurt rather than help me. I read in the New Testament that I should love my neighbor as myself. But do I really want everybody to love *me* as they love themselves? People love themselves in the strangest ways.

I know people whose sole purpose in life is to make as much money as they can and to have as much influence as they can. They call that loving themselves. It seems to me they get their values mixed up. "What does it profit a man if he does gain the whole world and lose his soul?" If that person said he wanted to love me the way he loves himself, I wouldn't take his friendship as a gift. I don't want to be like him.

What kind of friends give life a lift? Albert Schweitzer gave up a great academic career. A dream house in the suburbs did not interest him. Instead he plunged into the African bush helping sick helpless people. Why does his life arouse such different feelings in me than that of John Paul Getty with his massive fortune and art collection, his mansion—Sutton Place—set in a thousand acres of rolling hills bordered by trees and well-manicured hedges? What's the difference between the two? What really matters in life?

Suddenly I think I hear the Lord saying, "Art, you're looking for real friends? What are you looking for? Sit down a minute and write what you hope to find in such people. Then I'll see what I can do. I know everybody, you know."

So I sit down and start making my list. As I finish I sense the Lord again standing at my shoulder and saying, "Art, that's a good list." He runs his eye down the whole column. "That's the kind of person you're looking for?"

"Right, Lord. You know where I can find people like that?"

"Art, everyone in the world wants a friend like that. Why don't you let yourself become this kind of person? Let people find in you the friend they're looking for."

"Lord, you don't understand. I'm the one looking for a friend."

"I know, Art, so is everybody else. If you start letting yourself become this kind of person they'll be so happy to find you, you'll be swamped.

"Everyone looks for someone who cares about them enough to forget their own self-interest. What is a maturing Christian supposed to be? What is he supposed to do? Be a friend. At least that. You may not have all the answers, but at least you'll be headed in the right direction. And after all, it's direction not distance that counts.

"Few people have the courage to mature unless someone believes in them. Strictly rational solutions only apply to rational issues. It's much easier to repair a space ship than to mend a broken heart. Learn how to meet people at the place where they've given up. Become aware of what's really happening to them. Soak up details like a boy discovering a new neighborhood. Some have withdrawn into themselves. But every now and then you can see them look out from behind their protective shells. They feel cut off, uncared for. Before they'll ever develop as open, sincere, loveable persons someone has to love them deeply and boldly."

David found that kind of friend in Jonathan. I sense the depth of that friendship in one graphic sentence, "Jonathan strengthened David's hand in God." Surely that's the greatest thing one person can do for another.

Dizzy Dean will never go down as a great theologian of the twentieth century. Why should he? But he gave us some great baseball and his own brand of grammar and one of my favorite illustrations. Hoover Rupert tells of reading in the *Baseball Digest* about the time Dizzy Dean, in conversation with a reporter, called Howard Ehmke, a Philadelphia Athletics pitcher, a "fiddle hitcher." The reporter asked Dean what he meant.

"Well now," said Dean, "a 'fiddle hitcher' is a guy who has been up in the major leagues a long time and has lost his stuff so he takes to 'fiddle hitching' to get the batters out. He's the guy who fiddles around hitching up his trousers, pullin' at his cap, kickin' the dirt, anything to get the batter riled."

I think about how many people I run into who remind me of that pitcher trying to fiddle hitch their way through life. They are so unsure of themselves they try almost anything to psych me out. We get to talking about a subject the person knows nothing about. He'll pull a quote out of the air and with a long-winded argument make my ideas on the subject sound silly and his ideas like the wisdom of the ages. He knows how to get me so riled I explode and walk off leaving him king of the hill.

Or there's the person who finds his faith wearing thin.
He gropes for direction. He finds himself in a spot he
could have handled easily ten years ago. But now, as Dizzy
Dean would say, "He's lost his stuff." So he starts fiddle
hitching. And it works for a while. Then all of a sudden
everybody knows he's lost his stuff and a series of hits
knocks him right out of the box.

At that point in life people need other people who care
for them enough to "strengthen their hands in God." In
ways that I cannot explain such people speak for God to
me. I need them.

Maybe some feel they can maintain a Christian lifestyle
on their own without the support of Christian friends. I
can't. I need the uplift of a community that cares about me
if I'm going to make it.

Jesus makes that kind of difference in my life. He did
most of his work where people lived—on the streets, on
the docks, in places of business, and people's homes—not
in church. Usually whenever he went to church he got
into trouble. He once cracked "Where you see the vul-
tures you will find the body." Big crowds impressed Jesus' disciples—five thousand here, four thousand there.
They didn't impress Jesus. He knew a crowd could gather
for a bad reason as well as a good one. He put his faith
in a small group of people who cared deeply about each
other. He said. "I no longer call you servants, I call you
friends." And even when Judas betrayed him he still
called him, "Friend." That's Christianity. That's real living. A saving friendship!

G. H. A. Studdart-Kennedy told once of standing alone
at night on a moor beside the sea. Over him hung the gray

dark vault of heaven and a million stars. He couldn't hear a thing except the crash of the surf against the cliffs.

As he stood looking into the darkness and listening, his mind went back to an experience of World War I. He lay one night in a hole between the lines, miserable and soaking wet. He suddenly looked up and saw a form moving toward him in the darkness. He couldn't tell if it was a friend or an enemy. And he said to himself, "Suppose I call, 'Who goes there?' would the answer be silence or the word *Friend*?"

As that memory washed over him he came back to reality of the night on the moor. Standing alone with his thoughts he searched the darkness. And he said he sensed Someone other than himself moving out there in the vastness of creation. He wondered, "Suppose I call out 'Who goes there?' Would I get any answer? Or would there be silence and the crashing of the waves on the cliffs and the whisper of the wind through the heather?"

He decided to take a chance. He shouted out in the night, "Who goes there?" And he says, "I got my answer. I have sometimes doubted it. I've never wholly understood it. If I lost it I think I'd lose my soul. And I've been trying to say it ever since. That night I heard deep within me one word, *Friend*!"

That's who's behind it all—a great friend who loves us and gave himself for us, someone who in an uncalculating way cares about what happens to us. And every now and then I catch a reflection of him in the lives of people who in one way or another show me that they care for me like that.

5 *The Original Love/Hate Relationship*

I have lived long enough to know I have some personal enemies. Of course, paranoia will see an enemy in every face. But it's also sick to assume everyone will like me. Not everyone's heart skips a beat when I walk into the room. Some people just simply do not like me. I know some neighbors who watch for the worst in me because they love to see me get what they think is coming to me. How do I react when a man who smiles to my face pulls the rug out from underneath me behind my back? My response is usually typical—I tend to love my friends and hate my enemies.

Then along comes Jesus and tells me if I want to live before I die I must love my enemies and pray for those who despitefully use me. That statement comes close to heading the list of controversial sayings of Jesus. Sure Jesus loved his enemies. But look what happened! They killed him. Justice and mercy make some people furious. And I find myself saying, "Lord, what do you mean?

The Bible itself says in Ecclesiastes 3:8, there is 'a time to love and a time to hate.' "

And then I seem to hear the Lord saying to me, "Yes, Art, that's the Bible. There is a time to love and a time to hate. But, Art, your timing's off. You waste time loving things that God hates and hating people God loves. No one who loves God can at the same time love lying or economic exploitation or racism or war. And unless people begin to hate such evils and injustices they go from bad to worse. Centuries ago Amos hated to see powerful interests squeezing the life out of people. And in your own country not so long ago Abraham Lincoln hated what he saw slavery doing to the lives of slaves and slaveowners. You see, Art, if you really know God you will hate the evils that destroy the lives of people God loves. But if you say you love God and still hate your brother, you're a liar."

So I struggle to get my hands on what he's driving at—love persons, hate evils. That's the original love/hate relationship. Somewhere on the threshold of mid-life that idea took possession of the mind and heart of Jesus. Where did he get that idea?

I don't know for sure. I do know that his most famous ancestor, David, came up with the same idea centuries earlier. As he entered his thirties David's life hung by a thread. King Saul at the head of three thousand crack federal troops chased him to the south end of the Dead Sea, a place called "the Haunt of the Wild Goat." There David hid in a cave with about six hundred assorted malcontents, felons and hangers-on. Suddenly the king stood at the cave entrance. But because of the darkness he couldn't see David and the others hiding in the interior. The long chase of an outlaw across the desert had taken the starch out of Saul. So he lay down in the cool of the cave for a nap.

What a golden opportunity. David had him! Now's your chance, David. Kill him. Get rid of your enemy. That's the way he'd treat you.

That's the spirit I sense loose in the cave. And that's the spirit I sense loose in my world today—get rid of your enemies. I think if we had to depend on public opinion we'd still have public hangings. That dark chaotic mood colors my view of capital punishment, war, the treatment of prisoners and many other issues.

The theory sounds so practical. But suppose using force on my enemy will simply make him double up his fist and fight me harder, if he can. Suppose I reap what I sow? Then if I sow to the wind I will reap a whirlwind.

So I watch David in the darkness. Without a sound, dagger in hand, he creeps up on Saul. Then suddenly it looks like he's lost his nerve. Instead of cutting Saul's heart out he just cuts off the bottom of his outer robe.

After his nap, Saul wakes and leaves the cave. When he's gone a hundred yards or so David calls after him. He holds up the ragged piece of cloth. When Saul turns and sees it he understands in a flash what has happened. Tears well up in his eyes. And he says, "If a man find his enemy, will he let him go safe? So may the Lord reward you with good for what you have done to me this day."

I think I begin to see what it means to hate evil and love persons. *All Quiet on the Western Front* was perhaps the most moving story to come out of World War I. In one scene a soldier lies left behind in a shell crater. Suddenly a heavy body stumbles in next to him. The soldier spears the incoming person with his bayonet. But then he looks down at his fallen enemy and says, "Friend,

I didn't want to kill you, but you were only an idea to me before. An abstraction that lived in my mind. It was the abstraction that I stabbed. But now for the first time I see that you're a man like me. Now I see your wife and face and our fellowship. Forgive me, friend. We always see too late. Why do they never tell us that you are just poor devils like us? That your mothers are just as anxious as ours? That you have the same fears of death, and the same dying, and the same agony? If we threw away these rifles and uniforms, I could be your brother. And if I come out of this I shall fight the thing that struck us down."

Like so many, I grew up learning to fear my enemy, to hate him, and to plot against him. As a result I sometimes have a neurotic need to have an enemy. I need someone to blame when things go wrong. And I sense the same mood at work on a larger scale in national life. Sometimes nations need enemies to survive. They need someone to hate, someone to fear. They need someone to plot against to hold the country together. What chaos this problem fosters.

Watching David helps me understand how to go about loving an enemy and hating evil. For a long time I thought of "love" as warm feelings toward people. Usually attractive people stirred such feelings in me. But how do you work up warm feelings toward unattractive or hostile people? Usually that task is difficult for me. And maybe that's a good thing because warm feelings have a way of cooling off. I find they just don't have enough emotional fuel to keep burning and going for very long.

It took more than warm feelings to save Saul's life. David had a larger commitment—something that saved him from living at the mercy of his own feelings or at the mercy of how people felt about him. David believed his enemies were not necessarily God's enemies. As he said, "Who has ever lifted a finger against the Lord's anointed and gone unpunished," (1 Sam. 26:9). Yet how often do I feel that though God may love my enemies I just can't? I even doubt that David could work up genuinely warm feelings toward Saul.

But David did do something. If he could not control his feelings, he could control his behavior. I think that's why Jesus said, "Do good to them that hate you." He did not say, "Have warm feelings about them." He said, "Do something." That step takes conscious effort. It means choosing, deciding. David did something, and he did it regardless of how he felt about Saul.

Now I begin to see a little more clearly what loving my enemies means. It means doing what I can in my enemy's best interest. Often that has little to do with how I feel about him. I am free from feeling guilty about not having warm feelings toward arrogant, hostile people.

Columnist Sidney Harris tells of going with a friend to a newsstand. His friend gave the newsman a friendly greeting. But in return he got poor and discourteous service. He accepted the newspaper shoved at him, smiled and wished the newsman a nice weekend. As the two of them walked away from the newsstand Harris asked his friend, "Does he always treat you like that?"

"Always. The same every day."

"Well, are you always friendly and nice to him?"

"Yes, I am."

"But why when he treats you so badly?"

"Because I don't want him to decide how I'm going to act."

In this love/hate relationship I have a choice—I can

choose to let my enemies shape my character, or I can choose to let the love of God determine the shape of my life.

Will such behavior make a friend out of my enemies? Not necessarily. It didn't in David's case. It didn't always in the life of Jesus. And often it doesn't in mine.

And yet as I begin to behave as David did toward Saul, and Jesus did toward his enemies, I begin to sense something deep stirring within me, something I hadn't counted on. Such behavior gives God's love a chance to take root in my heart. It dawns on me that I know God's love, not by what others do to me or for me, but by what I do. In this sense my behavior becomes a means of grace, a way God has of helping me to live before I die.

Now the whole approach looks highly impractical, if by practical we mean what usually goes on in the world. Clarence Jordan, founder of Koinonia Farm, once commented, "Folks who love their enemies usually wind up on a cross like Jesus. They get slandered. Nobody would call this practical. And yet in its final stages unlimited love seems to be the only thing that can possibly make any sense. Crucifixions have a way of being followed by resurrections and the end of love seems to be at the beginning."

Jesus didn't tell me to love my enemies because it's practical. He told me to do it because that's how new life takes root in me. If God does not limit his love to those who love him, why should I? Yes, that may put me at the mercy of my enemies, but it will also give the Spirit of God a chance to shape my life so that I become like him.

Some years ago in a sermon I quoted Bertrand Russell. After the service a lady caught me and reprimanded me for quoting what she called "so evil a man." I know Russell does not even pretend to be a Christian, not by a long shot. But he did seem to look over his shoulder in 1950 in an address in New York City. He said this striking thing, "The root of the matter is very simple. An old fashioned thing, a thing so simple that I'm almost ashamed to mention it for fear of the derisive smiles with which wise cynics will greet my words. The thing I mean— please forgive me for mentioning it—is Christian love. If you have it, you have a motive for existence, a guide for action, a reason for courage, an imperative necessary for intellectual honesty."

6 ❧ Remember Who You Are

When asked to introduce myself I usually say something about my job or my family. I'm a minister, a husband, a lover, a father and a friend. Yet beneath these titles and these roles lives a person with a name. And who is he? "He never quite knew who he was," said Mrs. Willie Loman in *The Death of a Salesman*. I know the exact feeling. Sometimes I have trouble remembering who I am. My titles, my job, my sex shed little light on the question.

Joan Wixen, a well-educated intelligent woman who has just reached her forties, asks, "What do you do when your kids are grown and you discover your life is empty? Do you really have to come to the conclusion that you've been a slob all those years while your liberated friends have been out doing their thing? Suddenly it hits you. You wake up one morning all set to do things and discover there's nothing to do.

"Of course, there are some women who are perfectly content to put their energies full blast into P.T.A. or go all out for charities, and they accomplish something that way. And then, too, there are others who find satisfaction playing bridge a couple of times a week or going to the country club and working their energy out in a good game of tennis. There is no doubt in my mind that these are the lucky ones—the ones without this inner turmoil. The turmoil that some of us have tears us up inside because we feel we're a nobody unless we do something—something that says we're using our creative ability to the fullest and getting paid for it."

Most of us want our lives to count. We want to feel like a productive part of this world. But suddenly a lot of us start wondering if we'll ever find ourselves by simply performing a function or playing a role, even if we're getting paid for it.

A lot of us suffer a kind of spiritual amnesia. We have trouble remembering who we are. Some of that problem grows out of our feeling of isolation. It takes two persons in relation to each other to make humanity work. And when communication breaks down, the relationship begins to break up and inhumanity breaks out.

God has a great stake in all this. When people cannot speak to each other God loses one of his most effective means of speaking to us. We have an incarnation religion. God speaks most clearly through people and clearest of all in Christ.

A beautiful woman appeared in David's life. She was physically striking, intellectually sharp, warm and sensitive. Her husband, Nabal, had just two claims to fame—he drank a lot and he owned a lot of sheep. The fine combination of wealth and alcohol made him wonderfully arrogant. David, now an outlaw out in the hills with six hundred men, had to live off the land. So he asked Nabal for supplies. Regardless of how highly David phrased it, the request amounted to protection money. And as a matter of fact David's presence had protected Nabal's sheep from other marauding gangs. But Nabal answered, "I don't know who you are. And if you think I'm going to give anything to a common outlaw you've got another think coming."

So David, the man who spared the life of his great enemy, Saul, a few weeks earlier, strapped on his sword. "Never heard of the son of Jesse? Who does Nabal think he is? I'll teach him a lesson he'll never forget." With six hundred armed men David rounds the brow of the hill.

Suddenly he stopped. He saw another caravan coming toward him, and riding at the head of the procession was this beautiful woman, Abigail—Nabal's wife. She had loaded down the caravan with everything David needed and some luxuries besides. But she had more to give David than food.

David was armed to the teeth ready for blood; Abigail, unarmed but ready to talk. She had something to say that she couldn't prove, something she believed in spite of all the evidence to the contrary. If only David would listen.

Sometimes when I get excited and angry, my wife starts talking to me. And as she talks something begins to happen inside of me. Her words do things to me. It's like turning on the lights in a little dark room.

Jesus often talked to people just like that. A man came charging out of the graves with chains flaying from his wrists and from his feet and his eyes full of the devil. Jesus began to talk. He called out, "What's your name?" The man hesitated. No one had shown that kind of interest in him for years. As Jesus began to talk the man started to calm down. With words Jesus freed him from the devils that tore him apart, and the man began to get his head together. Soon he sat there in his right mind. So often some-body has to say something.

Abigail began, "David, remember who you are. What my husband said has put blood in your eye. Forget that for a minute and try to see yourself against the backdrop of a larger scheme of things. David, remember your frame of reference. Do you remember the oil running down your forehead when old Samuel appointed you heir to the throne? And can you remember the earth shaking beneath your feet when Goliath fell? You're a great person, David. You can be greater. Years from now you won't want to regret taking it out on us for our stupidity. You never re-gret any evil you don't do."

With words Abigail tried to get David to see himself and Nabal in the light of God. So often I need that kind of broad background. I need a larger frame of reference to get a handle on who I am in my immediate situation. Things happen to me that tend to blot out the whole hori-zon, things like a death in the family. Suddenly the crisis of the moment looms so large I can't see anything else. And yet such moments often become reminders of who I am.

Joseph Pintuara wrote in *Alive Now*, "I remember one hour and the only maple tree that we had had begun to make that yellow-green lace one April day when my mother died.

"My father was a carpenter. He had to carry his tool box all the way home from work, and he stood pale and puffing and they told him, 'Too late.' but when he saw her his face lit up and the color came back as if suddenly he'd told himself, 'Nothing drastic has happened. Just this.' She was no stranger to him even dead. Her familiar face made him safe from his confusion as if she had actually told him, 'I died. That's all.' He slightly raised his hands and said, 'Liz, I'm sorry I'm late.' Tears came, and that was it. And he held her hand.

"It was then for the first time I saw them as they really were. She, who I once knew as the beginning of everything warm and soft, my only real absolution for everything, was just a girl in a blouse with a lace collar whose name he couldn't guess. And he was a handsome boy with blonde hair, and they met at Coney Island one afternoon."

Suddenly seeing a larger frame of reference gives perspective to the immediate. I often need that. I need it not just in the great crises in life; I need it all the time!

In our home we live so close together that sometimes an offhand remark by one member of the family gets blown all out of proportion. Before you know it the tension fills the whole horizon as though it were an earth-shaking tragedy. Sometimes at such moments a sense of humor helps put a trifle in its place.

I once read of a husband and wife who went on an automobile trip. As they drove they fell into a super argument. Finally they just quit talking. They drove for miles through the country. Suddenly they passed a pasture where some long-earred mules stood grazing. The husband, breaking the silence, pointed to the mules and said, "Relatives of yours?" "Yes," she countered, "on my husband's side." A little humor cleared the air.

So Abigail talked to David. "David, forget my husband's stupid remark. Remember who *you* are in the light of God's purpose. 'The Lord had restrained you from shedding blood and giving vent to anger.'" She didn't ask him to deny that he had strong feelings. She asked him to recognize that when feelings run away with a person,

especially when tired, angry, or frightened, a person tends
to forget who he is. I do. My voice gets tense. My tongue
works faster than my brain. As my inner confusion
mounts, the louder I shout arguments defending inde-
fensible positions and behavior. The weaker my position
the harder I fight. Abigail appealed to that half-forgotten
part in David that reflected God's own heart.

I remembered standing once in a jewelry store waiting
to get my watch fixed. I noticed a collection of figurines
on the shelves. One in particular caught my eye. It was
two figures dressed in judo costumes locked in combat.
Grim intensity shown on their faces. I thought of how
much that resembles my inner conflicts. Part of me takes
off for the east and the other part heads west. That's not
always bad, but I do have to recognize the strong opposing
feelings I have inside of me. The trick is to get those feelings to work for me.

Why does the earth swing in its orbit in a way that
contributes to life? It is because of the balancing pull of
strong forces of gravity against each other. That's what
Abigail pleaded for—not that David deny the strong feelings at work inside of him, but that he make a conscious
effort to get those feelings to work for him and the humanization of his life as it fit into the purposes of God.

"If men rise up to pursue you," Abigail said to David,
"and seek your life, your life shall be bound up into the
bundle of the living and care of the living God." Behind
those words I hear the Lord saying to me, "Art, remember
that God has bound himself up into the bundle of life with
you. And he has not pulled out. He has a great plan and a
place for you and great work for you to do. Live in the
light of that framework of reference rather than by the

conditions of the moment. Try to anticipate what God has for you. He's out in front of you calling you to follow him. And he brings the future to meet you. Nothing can prevent the arrival of God's truth in God's time. God determines your future."

Now that framework of reference—that God has bound himself up in the bundle of life with us—clears up a lot of confusion and contradiction. Because he had that kind of perspective, Martin Luther King could speak of his dreams when nothing in present reality supported them. The night before his assassination he spoke of Moses and the prospect that he, like Moses, just might not reach the promised land. He remembered how Moses and the Israelites set out with only the promise that God would go before them. That perspective helped Martin Luther King dream dreams that present reality denied. That kind of remembrance fired his life with imagination and purpose.

To remember that God has taken that stance is a powerful truth! It helps deepen and broaden my perspective. It helps me get hold of my feelings. Who am I? I am a man loved by God. A man for whom Christ died. A person with a place in God's plan and real work to do. That's who I am. And that's who you are.

7   *Down But Not Out*

"Everybody sings the blues sometimes, everybody knows the tune." A man in his late forties slouched next to me on the couch. He was a productive man, a high achiever, the pastor of a large church. Yet I heard him saying, "I feel I've been a copier all my life. I haven't created anything on my own. And I feel the pressure of a job that requires continual public approval."

As he continued to talk to me I heard behind his words a man who suddenly realized he would not get done all he'd hoped to do. Nor would he become all he hoped to be. He sounded depressed as though something very crucial had suddenly gone out of his life.

I know how that feels. I know the anger and fear that churn inside a person in a moment like that. But I also know that if I use my psychic energy to feed my anger and my fear I could "break down." I could die before I live.

The strong often feel weak. The wise do not always have the answers. The brave sometimes lack courage. Maybe some people of iron can take the wear and tear of life undamaged, yet surely the rust worries even them.

Depression often comes close on the heels of great joy. So often depression strikes the day after a triumphant success as though my human nature cannot stand the strain of excessive good feeling. I get the job or the promotion or I make the deal. You'd think I'd feel on top of things for weeks. But in two or three days I can slide down into the depths of despair.

Many of us work at jobs that bore us limp. They feel like little more than routine hack work. Yet to most people, most of the time doing a good job at anything feels like that—routine hack work. The best work in the world usually feels like depressing hack work to the person doing it. Joseph Conrad in a letter to Edward Garnett in 1938 wrote, "I sit down for eight hours every day; sitting down is all. In the course of that writing day of eight hours I write three sentences which I erase before leaving the table in despair. Sometimes it takes all my resolution and self-control to keep from butting my head against the wall. I want to howl and foam at the mouth." That's hardly a pep talk for an ambitious young writer. We must realize that some lack of enthusiasm or boredom is perfectly normal and says nothing about the quality of performance.

Once again David comes to mind. God made some great promises to him. He promised him the kingdom. But David had little to show for it. He once complained, "One of these days Saul will kill me. I'll die before I receive the kingdom. God, you've bitten off more than you can chew. Why do you stand so far off, O Lord? I'll never be king."

Like a lot of the rest of us he felt he would never achieve what he had hoped to achieve, never be the man he hoped to be. He would die before he lived.

And I think Jesus knew that same feeling. When the crowds diminished toward the end of his ministry, he said to his closest friends, "Will you also leave me like the rest?" It looked like so many had completely dropped out of his ministry.

To be sure the degree of despair varies for different people. Some of us know we will not live as long as we already have. And it suddenly looks like things will not turn out alright. It feels like no matter how frantically I try I will not build my kingdom before death gets me. The incompleteness of my life tenses me up. A lot of people feel this way most of the time.

All kinds of things can get me down. I can't stay up all night and feel like singing "O What a Beautiful Morning" the next day—especially if on that morning I get loaded down with work and know I've got a committee meeting in the evening. And it doesn't help at all to have someone say, "Art, God will help you." I'd be better off taking a nap.

A lot of us don't eat the proper foods for good nutrition. I'm part physical and part spiritual; one affects the other. A rundown body invites a rundown spirit. A chemical imbalance can put me into an emotional power dive.

Furthermore, the tyranny of an accelerated life gets me down. When it does I begin to worry about my job, my health, and growing old. I suddenly sense I can't manipulate people well enough to have them satisfy my needs for achievement. I wonder if I'm losing my grip.

Even more confusing is the fact that sometimes I do succeed. I do exactly what I set out to do, but it leaves a taste of ashes in my mouth. I had counted on that achievement to meet my deep personal needs. But the success does not make me the man I thought it would. So I suffer what some call the "third act syndrome." I've raised the children, functioned reasonably well in society. Now, what do I do for an encore? Where have I misread the world and myself?

Feeling lonely also gets a lot of us down. I recently sat next to a man who was about to turn fifty. He was a man of wide influence whose children were grown and married. He said that when he and his wife married thirty years ago she shared his professional interest, though sometimes she resented the hours that kept him away from her and the family. But he always told her that he wanted her to have an identity of her own. Now, years later, she has that identity and a confidence in her own profession. And suddenly he finds himself emotionally unprepared to cope with what he had always said he wanted for her. "I still love her deeply," he said, "and she loves me. But I feel so terribly lonely. I feel unable to feed her emotional needs."

That man suddenly felt as though something had dropped out of his life. People can come to moments in their lives where they live together in families and yet feel they don't belong anywhere. There are many parents who can't communicate with children, children who can't get through to parents, and wives and husbands who rarely speak. Other examples of these people are lonely widows and pensioners condemned to confinement simply for growing old, the shy, the beaten, the ashamed, and the bewildered.

Furthermore nothing gets me down quite so much as feeling that God has gone into hiding. I look for him in nature and think I see his signature in the sunset. But that handwriting quickly blurs because of nature's moral indifference. Did the God who said, "Let there be light," also say let there be cancer, let there be pollution, let there be war? A tornado roars through the Midwest and kills good people and bad people alike. When I look for God in nature I get a confused picture.

So I look for him in events. But that gives no clearer picture. Might often triumphs over right. The race goes to the swift and the battle to the strong. Truth is on the scaffold and wrong on the throne. Christ is on the cross and Caesar in the palace. Sometimes it looks like God doesn't know what side he's on.

Once in a while late at night I'll turn on one of the "religious" television channels. The people on it talk as though they had God all figured out. They have an answer, usually a pretty neat one, for every question that comes up about God. And then I remember how the Jews in the first century thought they had God's Messiah all figured out. They expected him to come in like a conquering hero and rescue the nation politically. So when Jesus lay in a manger, and hung on a cross, they missed the presence of God. God came and went and they never knew it, simply because they had their own vision of the way God ought to come and the way God ought to act. But suppose God's ways are not our ways, and his thoughts are not our thoughts. Perhaps if I stop telling him what he ought to do, I might discover what he's doing.

Yes, sometimes life gets me down. But I know one thing about my moods—they change. And remembering that fact takes the terror out of some of my downers. Like the weather, my moods vary from day to day. God never promised to make me happy every day. Nor can life or the devil keep me permanently down. Dark moods, like dark clouds, come to pass. I may be down, but I am not out.

It's just that when one of those dark clouds passes over nothing feels worse than to have someone say, "Art, snap out of it." I'd like to, but I can't. I have about as much control over my low moods as I have over a storm front that blows into Los Angeles from Alaska. I can change my mind, I can change my behavior, but I have a great deal less control over my moods. I don't think it's wrong to feel angry or depressed. What counts is how I cope, how I face these feelings. Very often when a dark storm front moves through it clears up the weather and leaves better weather behind. It helps if I remember that.

What can I do when I'm down? Well, I do not look for people who will give me advice. I look for people who will listen to me. Having recognized the power of words I also recognize that a lot of us talk too much. Dietrich Bonhoeffer once commented, "Anyone who thinks his time is too valuable to spend keeping quiet will eventually have no time for God or his brother but only for himself and his own follies."

I think of Job, a man who lost everything—his family, his position in society, his business. And he had plenty to say about it. He had some real grievances against God, and he wanted to get them off his chest. Words poured out of him like water bursting out of a dam.

But did anybody listen? No. The God-fearing people of the day felt they had to defend God with some theological arguments, the kind of arguments that made Job feel he deserved everything he got. Job didn't need nor did he want such advice. He said, "Ah, if you would only be silent and let silence be your wisdom." But his friends prattled on with their condescending chatter and dressed it all up in pious words. When they stopped for a breath, Job pleaded, "Listen to me, just listen to me and let that be the comfort you offer." But he knew that even if they kept quiet for a few minutes they weren't listening. They simply filled in the time thinking of a new set of arguments—all for his own good, of course! Finally Job couldn't take it any longer. He burst out, "How futile is the comfort you offer me! How false your answers ring."

What do I need when I'm down? I need someone who will really listen and not have one eye on the door. I noticed in a recent survey that 40 percent of the wives in America feel their husbands do not listen to them. Thirty-six percent of these wives thought their husbands were much too sensitive to even innocuous criticism often interpreting it as an attack. And 34 percent of the wives felt much better talking things out with a friend than they did with their husbands. One wife said, "He listens to me as if I were a not-too-bright child, and I get angry." Another said, "Sex is the only communication that interests my husband." And a third said, "Whenever I start talking about anything my husband accuses me of nagging." Now of course a lot of trouble develops between people when we hold each other responsible for every word we say in a burst of anger. It's strange how a lot of us assume that we know what's going on in the minds or hearts of our husbands or wives. The fact is we don't.

Two couples got together to play "Forty-two." After they had dealt the dominos one of the husbands noticed his wife trying to catch his attention. She rolled her eyes and looked down her face in a peculiar way. He thought surely she had a great hand. So he bid. She didn't have anything, and they lost. When the next deal came he noticed his wife obviously trying to get his attention again. This time she lifted her hand to her cheek. He thought obviously since her last signal meant she had a bad hand, she must have a great hand this time. So he bid with a vengeance. To his horror he discovered she had another bust hand. In the painful discussion after they got home, she told him she only wanted to let him know he had a gob of shaving creme on his cheek. Two people living close to-. gether can assume they know what is in the mind and heart of each other and really have no idea. A crucial part of communication is learning to listen.

Jesus had a knack for listening, and people felt it. He listened not only to their words but to the tone of their voice, the look in their eyes and the gestures that they made with their bodies. As he listened, amazing changes began to take place in people's lives. People don't change because someone tells them to; they change as someone listens. One afternoon Jesus spent maybe three hours listening to Zacchaeus. So far as we know Jesus didn't say much. But when Zacchaeus got through talking everything out, Jesus said, "Salvation has come to this house today" (Luke 19:2). Zacchaeus' whole life began to change.

So when David felt God had let him down, he cried, "Out of the depths I cry to thee, Lord, hear my voice." After he exhausted his arguments and ran out of everything he had to say, he came to a point where he was able to hear. The thing that God does for me, the thing that gets under the load of my life, is his ability to listen and take me seriously.

And I've run into a lot of unhappy people who don't

need food or clothes or a house or money or comfort or advice. They need to feel that someone can hear them. I see it in my children. How often I say, "Son, listen to me," before I ever listen for his point of view or opinion. And I see that same thing in my friends and in my critics. Suddenly all these people seem to say, "Art, listen to me, just listen to me, and let that be the comfort you offer."

So when the bottom drops out I look for someone who will hear me. In the process I begin to breathe the atmosphere of a new life. I come to the point where I can say, "Lord, handle these dark moods of mine until I get the courage and strength to handle them myself."

When I get down I sometimes listen for the wind. The wind reminds me of how God works. It reminds me of that dawn breeze on Easter morning. All through the chaos and complexities of life, God's Spirit continues to work. And even on the blackest night if I open my window I can hear just a faint rustle of the wind reminding me God has neither gone to sleep nor lain down on the job.

No one can control God any more than anyone can control the wind. The wind blows where it wants to. And God will go where he wants to and do what he wants to do. Men always try to limit him to a particular sphere of influence as though he could not make a way of salvation outside of their ideas of how he ought to operate. God forever blows through those ideas and blows them over. The wind blows not where the timid or the dogmatic say it ought to blow. It blows where it wants to blow. And if I try to shut the door against it, it will blow the door down as it did Easter morning when men thought they had sealed away God's Christ forever.

I like to race sailboats. In sailing you can't always tell

where the wind will take you, which sets me to thinking that I cannot always tell where the Spirit of God will lead me. Now that frightens some people. But it encourages a lot of the rest of us, because it means we cannot tell what God may yet make out of our lives. No matter what gets me down I can never say, "I've had it. I've gone as far as I can go. I've thought as much as I can think. I've done as much as I can do. There's not a chance that anything great can happen to me and my circumstances at this point of life." I can never say that unless I want to make a liar out of God himself. I may be down, but I'm not out "if" the Spirit of God dwells in me. "Behold I am making all things new" (Rev. 21:5).

8 ⟩ *When Things Fall Apart*

Things have a way of falling apart. Take Jim, for example. He had everything going for him when he started with the company. Promoted three times in quick succession, he bought a new house. The first baby came and then the second, and he and Ann thought of a third.

Then suddenly during a routine medical checkup the doctor discovered cancer. Jim went into the hospital and had surgery. They told him they'd got it all. And after two years Jim seemed stronger. He felt and looked better than ever.

But twice in the past year the company passed him over for promotion. The personnel managers said they wanted to make sure about his physical condition. Could he take the additional responsibility? What would the pressure do to him? So Jim sat there for a year and watched other men whom he felt were less qualified pass him up.

And after that happened about six times he began to fall apart inside. When he came home at night the smallest family hassle drove him deeper into despair. He felt his family didn't understand him either. His children made too many demands on his thought, energy, time, and money.

His wife didn't understand his frustration. And he felt powerless to get himself together. As Paul Valerie once said, "The trouble with the world is that the future is not what it used to be."

Dreams get broken. So do promises and relationships. When life begins to fall apart, what then?

David once came to a moment when everything had gone wrong. Saul had driven him into the arms of the archenemies of his people, the Philistines. David found himself marching with the Philistines against his own people. Try to imagine Moshe Dayan, eye patch and all, suddenly at the head of an Egyptian tank corps moving across the Suez. That's the position David found himself in. And many of the Philistines didn't trust him for a minute. As they approached the battle they decided to send him back to Ziklag behind their lines. But when David got home he found a deserted heap of smoking ruins. Everything was gone—wives, children, property and cattle. David's best friends suddenly picked up stones to kill him on the spot. They'd had enough.

David chose that moment to "strengthen himself in the Lord his God." But what in the world does that mean?

When things start to fall apart I may think of God but not think too highly of him. I'm like the soldier, fatally wounded an hour before the cease-fire, who said "Isn't it just like God to do a thing like this to me?" I react as though God went around the world starting wars, letting cancer loose, and sending all kinds of misery and evil into life, behaving like some strict, demanding, vindictive autocrat. No wonder a lot of people get fed up with religion. Who in his right mind could believe in a God like that?

And I have a feeling that many who say, "I don't believe
in God anymore," really mean, "I don't believe in *that*
God anymore."

Apparently David thought of God in terms of encour-
agement and strength. Life fell apart; he had nothing—no
family, no city, no home, no money, and very little faith.
Nothing was left except God—just God. Is that enough
to face life with?

Jesus went around opening people's eyes. When the disciples of John the Baptist asked him, "Where do you
live?" Jesus answered, "Come and see." And he didn't
mean "come and see a geographical place." He meant
"come and see how the world looks to me. I want to open
your eyes to a whole new set of facts." Life has a way of
crowding out that kind of vision. And when it does, life
becomes a push button affair with very few glad surprises
and no great wonders, just a commonsense, down-to-earth
approach that quickly gets thin, flat and stale.

Then all of a sudden for no apparent reason, a man
will see an ordinary bush on fire with God as Moses did
out in the desert. Suddenly another order of reality forces
itself into his thinking. People always have trouble nailing
down what they see in words. All the standard clichés
don't satisfy me. I'm sure they won't satisfy you. But people like David and Moses lived as though they saw the
invisible God. There are some people today who have that
kind of vision. They see things that cannot be and yet are,
things that can't be photographed or measured in technical
terms. Those people who have it live today fully but they
never live for today. They have a way of seeing life that
goes above, beyond, and around all the days. Such people

point to things that belong to a larger world as though they see someone behind the scenes who helps them through life and gives them cues for the hard lines.

In this sense I believe David strengthened himself in the Lord his God. I remember years ago standing one night out under the stars. It was for me a time of confession and commitment. I remember the warmth of feeling accepted that night. And I sensed the Lord saying, "Art, you can forget about the past. I have. I'm for you." In the middle of the whole experience I felt a great calm that I still can't express or describe adequately. And now years later when things start falling apart and my faith flickers, my mind goes back to that moment, and I try to remember how the world looked then and how I felt then. I try to catch sight again of that other set of facts and remember that God goes right on believing in me. And like David I strengthen myself in the Lord my God.

God comes close to us all in many surprising ways. And in those moments we catch a glimpse of facts beyond the ordinary, commonsense facts by which we usually live. What a terrible waste to forget those moments, to forget those visions, to ignore them, to distrust them or fail to make use of them. What a terrible waste if I forget how life looks in those flashes when God seems so terribly close and my fellow human beings so wonderfully real and I know a love of things worth loving. Moments when I know a better world exists within me and around me. If I forget such moments of vision, I could die before I live.

So when it feels like life has begun to fall apart, the critical question remains, "Am I faithful to those moments of vision?" What's the greatest truth of my life—the way things look in those astonishing moments when I see a larger sort of reality or the way things look most of the rest of the time?

Once the Apostle Paul could say, "I have not been disobedient to that heavenly vision. I have lived in the light of it." In that same sense David strengthened himself in the Lord his God.

Now sometimes we need to hear painful truth about ourselves and about our society and about our world. But at other times we need reassurance. We need to see the glory of our Lord and the splendor and the sheer joy of his presence. And I'm beginning to discover that with most of us, one glimpse of that kind of glory sustains us far more than a lifetime of regretting or studying human sin.

So when life began to fall apart, David started to strengthen himself in his God. *His* God. What a difference a personal pronoun makes. What a world of difference between just plain God and *my* God. What a world of difference between girls and *my* girl. Not simply the God of Abraham, the God of Isaac, the God of Jacob, but my God. A personal God is the difference between a vague nominal religious feeling and a vital substantive sustaining faith. When David could no longer say "my city" or "my home" or "my wife" or "my friends" he could say "my God." And he found that to be enough. Dietrich Bonhoeffer centuries later commented, "I believe God will give us all the power we need to resist in all kinds of distress, but he never gives any in advance lest we should rely on ourselves and not on him alone."

And it looks to me as though Jesus came to a moment when the whole world seemed to fall apart on him. People had shouted his praises earlier in the week. They welcomed him like a conquering hero. But on that night out under the olive trees, no one, not even his disciples, understood. They had all missed the point. And maybe out there Jesus heard God the Father saying something like, "My Son, you don't have to worry about how things will turn out. You can leave that to me. Trust me with everything, including yourself."

And as I think about that story in the New Testament it looks like three times Jesus tried to argue God out of it. "Father, if there is any way you can take this cup from me." But he finally came to the point where he said, "Father, not my will, but thine be done."

The next day he went to the cross. And it looked like God had taken a vacation. And yet out of that grim business God brought the salvation of the world on Easter morning.

I believe if God can cope with the cross of Christ he can surely cope with mine. Strengthening my life in God when everything starts falling apart does not mean whistling in the dark to keep my courage up. It's the ability in those moments to see that greater is he who is in us than he who is in the world. And surely that is the faith that overcomes the world.

9 *Out of Patience*

Out of patience! Stalled freeway traffic, a three minute delay in the kickoff of a big game—they'll do it to me every time. When the movie gets out of focus in the theatre I feel like joining the other handclappers, whistlers and footstompers. I'm part of an impatient society, an impatient time, an impatient people. I like instant coffee, instant TV warmup, and direct distance dialing.

And impatience has a lot to do with shaping our society. Impatient people facing a problem demand action. They hope bold, aggressive action will win them the reward of living happily forever after. Impatience worked wonders when Americans faced nonhuman nature. With bulldozers we move mountains in record time. Unfortunately we bulldozed a lot of flora and fauna with the same impatience with which we treated the rocks. We cut down forests and exterminated the buffalo and killed and corralled the Indians.

Still impatience does have virtues. A time comes when you have to quit talking and act. A patient's fever does not go down simply because the doctors discuss his case. The patient could die if they don't act.

But today as Marshall McLuhan points out, "Technology has shrunk our world to the dimensions of a small town. And suddenly in the back alleys of that small town, we Americans have run into problems that simply do not respond to our traditional impatient treatment." Historian Arnold Toynbee cautions us saying, "You could get rid of the problem of the Sioux Indians and perhaps live happily forever after in South Dakota. But you can never come to the end of the Russians or the Chinese."

But I am impatient. I'm impatient with irresponsibility. I'm impatient with injustice. I'm impatient with imperfection. I'm impatient with myself. Yet while I get impatient with myself and my children I often remain relatively patient with friends and co-workers. And I know people who love and understand their children but get terribly impatient with God. They want quick permanent answers, no more delay, no more nonsense. If impatience works wonders in moving mountains, why not in the development of human nature? We could die before we live.

Ever so often someone comes in to talk with me hoping to solve the hangups of a lifetime in half an hour or less. A woman harboring such hopes came to Cecil Osborne once. She had gone through a series of marriage castastrophes. But the pattern seemed to repeat itself. She asked him how long it would take her to work through some of her difficulties. He said, "Well, there is no way to tell. Maybe a year, maybe three years, maybe five years depending on a lot of factors." "Five years!" she answered. "Great Scott, I'll be forty-five by then." And Osborne asked, "Well, if you do nothing, how old will you be in five years?" "Okay," she laughed, "when do we start?"

It didn't take five years. But it took more than an hour or a week. People become whole very gradually, and despite many setbacks, and under the cross.

Nothing, absolutely nothing, in the Bible tells me faith in God will instantly solve my human problems. Yet a lot of today's preachers tell me that it will. But it certainly did not work out that way in the lives of many people in the Bible, certainly not in David's case.

Faced with defeat by the Philistines, King Saul committed suicide on Mount Gilboa. His son and heir, Jonathan, also died in the battle. And the Philistines spiked their headless bodies to the walls of Bethshan. "O prince of Israel laid low in death! How are the men of war fallen," cried David (2 Sam. 1:19). With the king and heir dead David began to wonder if he ought to act decisively, quickly, and take over the country. David inquired of the Lord as to the time to take the kingdom. And the Lord said, "Go." David said, "To which city?" And the Lord said, "To Hebron" (2 Sam. 2:1). And the men of Judah came there and they anointed David king over the house of Judah.

But aren't there twelve tribes in Israel? What about the other eleven and the rest of the country? David had only a tiny fragment of the people behind him, people from the deep South. Hadn't God promised him the whole kingdom? Why just Hebron? But there he sat for seven years.

Now it's really hard on a man of action to just sit and wait. Usually I feel when I'm not doing something, nothing is getting done. Waiting looks and feels like weakness rather than strength. So I take a closer look at David sitting around in Hebron for seven years. And suddenly I see something new and fresh about the nature of his God. When it comes to developing human nature, God takes his time. He doesn't push people around. He's patient.

I know people who do push people around. They usually look strong and dynamic. They do the talking. They make the decisions. And they get their way. And other people let them do it, because it's the only way you can relate to them.

But God does not prowl around the universe like a gigantic dictator snapping his fingers to get his way in a hurry. How often an impatient person like me wishes that he would. I want things done right now. I have a hard time relating to this patient aspect of God. In my experience, power and patience don't seem to go together. If one has the power why not act? If God is just, why should he put up with injustice anywhere in the universe for one split second longer? Why all the waiting?

The first Christians had trouble with this concept. A lot of them started dropping out of the church. They got impatient with God. Jesus made all those big promises about the kingdom of God on earth as it is in heaven. In fact, he said he'd come again to see that things got done just right.

But nothing happened! Everything seemed to go from bad to worse. So a lot of people just gave up on Christianity. "Where is the promise of his coming?" they asked. Things go on like they've always gone on. People lie and cheat as much as they have ever lied and cheated. What good is all this Christianity?

So the Apostle Paul wrote, "Here is one point, my friends, which you must not lose sight of: with the Lord one day is like a thousand years and a thousand years like one day. It is not that the Lord is slow in fulfilling his promise, as some suppose, but that he is very patient with you, because it is not his will for any to be lost" (2 Pet. 3:8–9). God waits for human nature to develop and he will wait a thousand years as though it were a day. His power shows up as patience. God does not use his power to push me around. He will wait for me to see the truth and to choose it and to do it.

Today people all over the world struggle to come to grips with what we call an energy crisis. We woke up a year or two ago and suddenly it felt like we had begun to run out of everything. But I started to thinking, how for billions of years, long before people ever appeared on earth, somehow nature stored up all kinds of energy in her basement. For thousands of years people didn't know anything about it. They shivered in cold, damp caves and houses not knowing what they had under their feet. Lakes of energy existed that nobody knew anything about. And even if they had known, they wouldn't have known what to do with it.

Not so long ago we burned gasoline as a waste product of kerosene. We just didn't know what to do with it at the time. Slowly we discovered new truth and new options. We've learned a little, and it has meant a lot. But we have a lot more to learn about appropriate technology and the gearing of consumption to a standard of sufficiency. And God has the patience to wait for people to make their own breakthroughs into the discovery of truth. After all who would want to live in a world with nothing left to discover?

Now suppose we carry that a little further into human nature. God promised David something that would fulfill him as a person. He promised him a kingdom—a kingdom of God. And Jesus talked about something like that. He said the kingdom of God is at hand. He meant great spiritual resources simply await my discovery. But God will not push them on me. He waits for me to make my own discovery in my own way. And he waits for me to choose freely "the way" as my way.

Impatient people feel uncomfortable with that idea. They believe that if God is God he would hurry up. If he is God, he'd get a move on. Why doesn't he bring his "way" in and put a quick end to the tyrants in business, school, and government? Why doesn't he make things happen? Why does he let events push him around?

We've all seen what happens to people who let life push them around. A man goes to his office and takes orders. He comes home and lets his family tell him what to do. He doesn't offer any opinions of his own. He just parrots the opinions others tell him. He makes no decisions. He simply reacts to the decisions others make. He never steps out first. He never takes the lead. Sometimes we all play the role of either the "pusher" or the "pushee." And sometimes a "pushee" who takes it on the chin all day at work comes home and acts like a poor man's Hitler with his family.

But I cannot fit God into my narrow definitions of "pusher" or "pushee." As I watch David waiting to inherit the kingdom, suddenly the whole Bible breaks open and I begin to see a quality of God I have never seen before. This God gives himself enough time not just to get people out of misery and boredom but to get the misery and boredom out of people. To do it he puts up with arrogance and bigotry and censoriousness and defiance and defensiveness. But never once does he use his power to drive people to their knees. He keeps waiting and hoping that some of them will see "the way" and some of them will catch on.

So when it comes to human nature, spiritual development takes time. And that discovery dawns slowly on the mind of man. It comes like the movement from darkness to predawn twilight and then the dawn. It takes time for it to dawn on me. And I've begun to see that many life-changing spiritual discoveries occur in mid-career. Suddenly what has always been there becomes part of my experience, and I step out of darkness into light.

I remember my first attempts as a child to grow some beans in the back yard. I dug up the ground, put in the beans, covered them over and watered them. The next morning I went out and looked. Nothing had happened. I went out each morning for two or three days; still nothing. So I started to dig up the beans to see if they were okay. I wanted to see how they were getting along. I never got a crop from that planting.

And that childhood experience helps me to see that life and growth in human nature takes time and patience. It's just that the word *patience* upsets the child in me that wants quick, no-nonsense results.

When I read the New Testament I see how Peter, James and John and the rest did not develop into mature human beings, let alone solid Christians overnight. Even after three years of constant living with Jesus they ended up at the Last Supper arguing like children about who would sit where. Within hours one of them betrayed him. And they all denied him. They said they would die for him, but they ran like rabbits when it really came down to that.

Now I know how weak and hard to live with I am.

But I believe God accepts me this way. That he loves me for what I am. When he made me, he knew what he was doing. How long should I attend church? A few weeks? Until I'm eighteen? A lifetime? I begin to realize how open ended my development is. I never arrive. And yet I'm always arriving. As Reinhold Niebuhr once commented, "There was a time when I had all the answers. My real growth began when I discovered the questions to which I had the answers were not the important questions."

So David waited seven years to allow God to prepare him to inherit the kingdom. And I remember how the prophet Isaiah wrote, "But those who look to the Lord will win new strength," (Isa. 40:31). If God has the patience to allow me to develop, why should I get impatient with myself? It will take time for all of us to arrive. That insight helps take some of the anxiety out of my life.

10 *In Times of Transition*

Some nights I can't sleep. I try one side and then the other. Nothing happens. In fact the harder I try the wider awake I feel. My watch glows in the dark. Have I just tossed and turned an hour? It feels like forever. So I get up and take an aspirin and repeat the process. The night drags on.

A lot of us, at the height of our powers, feel apprehensive. We've come to a time of transition. Hopes we had a few years ago have died. And yet life pushes us on. The weight of more and more and heavier and heavier responsibilities presses down upon us. One thing keeps coming right after the other. Chaotic pressures build up.

Some time ago representatives of a major network appeared before a Senate committee investigating television violence and crime. In trying to justify itself the network said that shows must have some terror in them, but that they ought not to go beyond "a tolerable tension."

That's a useful phrase—a tolerable tension. Life often seems shot through with both terror and tension, particularly in times of personal or national transition. What will keep either within tolerable limits?

85

A lot of us begin feeling cornered, trapped. We try diversionary tactics. We try to keep busy. But such diversions simply help us lose touch with ourselves and our world. Sooner or later a dense fog of apathy settles over everything. Nothing feels like much fun anymore. So a person keeps going through the motions of living when the heart has gone out of him. And that mood can become epidemic and grip the heart of a nation as well as the heart of an individual.

Governor Morris, United States Ambassador to the Court of Louis XVI of France, wrote to President Washington, "Louis XVI is a good man. In another generation he would have made a good king. The trouble is that he has inherited a revolution." Unfortunately Louis XVI came to the throne in a time of desperate transition. For years explosive pressures had built up. He didn't know how to release them gradually nor could he maintain the status quo.

It seems to me like we have come to one of those times again—a time of transition in personal life and community life. In so many ways my early years did not prepare me for what I now find. I have trouble getting hold of the real forces involved.

The *New York Times* a little while ago reported the publication of a new encyclopedia called, *An Encyclopedia of the Future*. The contributors include Dr. Werner von Braun, Marshall McLuhan, Herman Kahn, Arnold Toynbee, Edward Teller and a host of others. The members of the Hudson Institute in Paris, the European office of the internationally known thinktank headed by economist Edmund Stillman, head up the project. Stillman says, "We're not forecasting the twenty-first century. That can't be done." But he believes that most of the people who will read the encyclopedia, no matter how well-informed, really are not abreast of present reality. He says, "They are thinking ten to fifteen years in the past, laboring under the weight of outmoded ideas that simply do not correspond to present reality."

In times of great transition many familiar assumptions simply do not fit present reality. I begin to wonder if there is a future with me in it. Though I can't see the future it does affect me. Plants and animals all grow in relationship to an unseen future. An eggshell breaks open and a baby chick wobbles out into the sunlight. An acorn seedling through many years contorts itself slowly into a giant gnarled oak. Particularly in times of transition I continue to grow in relation to a future I cannot see. It's just that I have a hard time feeling worthwhile unless the direction in which I'm going and the things I do matter to someone. A preacher as well as a salesman, mechanic, administrator, teacher, or singer has to feel that what he does counts for something.

Sometimes I get terribly bored with myself. If only I could escape from me. Now and then I feel a powerful urge toward self-transcendence. Because of this urge in many people today, spiritual exercises, mystical theology and yoga as well as alcoholism and drug addiction are flourishing.

Faith will not release me from all tension and terror. But it can help me make a transition that leads beyond myself to God. And again I hear the voice of God speaking to me in and behind events in the life of David at a time of transition.

When David assumed his throne it marked a transition

in his life. And it came at a time of acute transition in the life of his people. Anthropologists have described that time as a transition from the Bronze Age into the Iron Age. King Saul, David's predecessor, had to borrow iron plows from the Philistines. But under David's son, Solomon, the Israelis had iron furnaces of their own to turn out tools and weapons.

A sociologist would point out the cultural conflicts of the time between the primitive Israelis and the sophisticated Philistines, those Phoenician traders who gave us our alphabet.

A political scientist would surely point to the transition toward centralized government. He would point out David's use of traditional religion to legitimize his coup d'etat and the power play he used to seize control and build his dynasty.

But the men who wrote the Bible had a way of seeing behind these genuinely historical insights. Behind these events they tell us they saw the activity of God. And that's what I want to see in my time of transition. I want to see the movement of God behind the events of my day. I want to see it in and behind the events of my life.

Out of the chaos following King Saul's defeat and death, David emerged as the strong man in the whole country. After seven years of bloody civil war he brought the country under his iron control. Under David the Israelis enjoyed the kind of unity that Spain enjoyed under Franco. But the Northern tribes of the country always remained restless. So restless were they that finally after the death of David's son, Solomon, they split off again. Tension and terror, assassinations and rebellions scarred David's entire reign.

And people of that time believed so many different things. The whole world found itself going through the transition from the Bronze Age to the Iron Age. So David suddenly came up with an idea he hoped would unite his people around his new capital, Jerusalem. He would bring the old symbol of Hebrew heritage, the ark of God's covenant, to the city. That wooden box the priests had carried all over the desert for forty years still made hearts beat faster. So David with dramatic ceremony and flair brought the ark to the capital.

Then he had a problem. Where would he put it? From his great cedar palace he looked out on that shabby delapidated tent in which the ark rested. Over the years the tent had begun to rot out and fall apart. So from his executive office David issued an announcement. He would build an appropriate house for God. And he told the leading preacher of the capital his intention.

Up to this point anyone can understand the story in terms of a clever politician trying to exploit the religious heritage of his people in order to win popular support. I understand that. I've seen plenty of it in my own day. I've heard political leaders who are personally inactive in their own churches make a great display of religion in order to gain popular support.

But suddenly the story in the Bible takes a dramatic turn. Through the preacher, Nathan, David receives an answer from God to his proposal to build a house. A flat no! God wanted no part of making any head of government look impressive.

God often says no. And he often says no to my highest hopes and fondest dreams. Moses wanted to lead the people into the land of promise. God said no. He had other plans. David wanted to build a temple. God said no. And suddenly I see that a lot of us will not live to see our fondest dreams fulfilled. Medical scientists may die before they see the secret of cancer solved. Artists will die with the perfect picture still unpainted.

A man goes into business with dreams of success—all for the glory of God, of course! But he runs into competition fiercer than he bargained for. Years pass and with them go some of his resilience and optimism. He knows he'll never make much of the business now. Or a woman who wants a home and children. But she has to go out and get a job and now feels she will walk a solitary road to the very end. Life simply will not always go our way. But does that mean we have failed? What has happened?

David had high hopes and the best of motives. Why should he live in a better house than the house that housed the presence of God? And I dream dreams and I have visions of what I think would honor God in my life and in the world. And many of my dreams may spring from the best motivation in the world. And yet sometimes God without explanation flatly says, "No, Art, that's not for you."

After all, God never asked David to build him a church. Years later David seemed to understand why. As he looked back he must have said, "The word of the Lord came to me saying, 'You have shed much blood in my sight, waged great wars. For this reason you shall not build a house in honor of my name. But you shall have a son, and he shall be a man of peace, and he will build a house to honor my name.'"

God often says no in order to help me see basic realities. When God says no in a time of transition he forces me to ask, "What kind of a person then does the emerging era require?" That's the basic question at any time of transition. A new era requires new people, new minds, clean hands. A new age requires a new vitality. Yes, God's house needed building. But David's hands dripped blood. The building of the house of peace required a new generation.

David's times required David. David and his generation prepared the way for Solomon and what Solomon's generation would accomplish.

That's the fact of life; I need to recognize it. Different times do call for different capacities and different kinds of people. We do live in different generations. There's nothing wrong with that. Humanity has lived through ages of reason, ages of discovery, ages of faith, and ages of industry. Each age has a particular kind of person. My sons and daughters need not see as I see or think as I think. Why should they? Once I recognize that, it takes a lot of pressure out of my life. I have a job to do. So do they. The jobs may be quite different in nature.

For centuries the Western world honored the Greek philosophers. Then in the transition years of the Middle Ages, the old Greek-Roman patterns gave way and the architect emerged with new styles of living and energy that sent great soaring cathedrals into the sky. Then in the sixteenth century artists took center stage—men like Michelangelo and Leonardo da Vinci. Then came nineteenth century England with persons of letters—Tennyson and Wordsworth, Thackeray and Dickens.

Each age required a particular kind of person. The industrial age gave us the banker, the businessman, the scientist and the technologist. These men have revolutionized our world in ways we haven't yet fully understood.

Now suddenly to a lot of us it feels like the means of

life have grown all out of proportion to our understanding of the ends of life. We have put so much time and effort into the making of wealth and power, on making things, buying them and selling them that we have created huge cities with tall buildings crowded with people, stuffed with energy consuming gadgets and machinery.

We had little time to think about factors that make for the humanization of life on this planet. It does no good to rebel against mechanization or technology. A particular era of human development demanded them. And I can't turn back the clock. Nor do I think God asks me to park my brains in order to save my soul. Surely God doesn't quarrel with scientific truth or technological discovery. He invented it all. Technology is neutral. It gives wings to my feet, puts power in my hands, takes so much drudgery out of my life.

It's just that today we have come to a transition. What is appropriate technology? Suddenly I face questions like, "Why should a top executive in an oil company demand a salary of over $150,000 while a teacher, who trains people to think, gets an average salary of around $9,000? What makes the driller of oil a significant person and the maker of persons an insignificant one? To what kind of person should we give honor and our most important awards?" I think about the enormous salaries paid to entertainers and athletes, and I remember the gladiators of old Rome— heroes while they lasted. I see the bone-rattling fullback who can crack the line and in a season earn more than a college professor earns in a dozen years.

So people tell me "small is beautiful" and "less is more" as though driving little shift cars, eating food without preservatives, living in spartanly heated homes, wearing natural fibers and giving up energy-guzzling appliances automatically makes for wholeness in life. Yet I can't believe we must deliberately try to return to poverty. We don't need more poverty in the world but better balance. And of course that may mean an adjustment in my lifestyle. Such an adjustment would not bring me anywhere near poverty. But will it make me whole?

I face the question David faced—what kind of persons do these times of transition require? What kind of persons will it take to make peace and justice on earth? Churchill once commented that a man who can win a war can seldom make the peace. And the men who can make the peace could not have won the war. I suppose he serves as his own best example.

It's no longer just the speed of change, now it's the scope of change that makes the job so difficult. And yet I have a feeling that what our times demand, the gospel has always promised. If new times need new persons Jesus apparently brings about such a change in people. "If any man be in Christ," said the Apostle Paul, "he is a new creature" (2 Cor. 5:17, KJV). He goes through a transition. Old attitudes, old styles of life, old ways of seeing things, old behavior begin to be sloughed off.

After Hiroshima, Norman Cousins wrote that modern man is obsolete. He's a misfit in a new world. He has leaped centuries ahead in making a new world but hasn't prepared himself to live in it. He's an old man in a new world. And now he has no option. He has changed the world so much he must himself begin to change to stay alive in it.

Our times of transition, I believe, demand persons of warmth and integrity. Enthusiastic religiosity and ethical integrity do not necessarily go together. An ethical person keeps his eyes open to realities that go beyond the range of technical competence and social expediency. He will explore the meaning of things and the purpose of existence.

Scientists brought us to this point by asking *how*. How does the universe work, how do things happen? And their answer to the question "how" has brought unbelievable changes.

But now the great questions have shifted from the *how* to the *why* of things. What's the use of knowing how to do something if you have no understanding of why you ought to do it? Why split the atom or conquer outer space if in the process we destroy human life?

So the great questions of this time of transition have become ethical and theological questions science never intended to answer. I begin to see how Jesus never passed over such questions in silence. As I try to follow him I begin to see that any effort in that direction has a future with me in it.

So, I see a period of transition as a period full of hope. DeChardin, that marvelous French philosopher and Christian, said, "We move into a painful crisis in the buildup of knowledge and the pressure in human life will not lead to a breakdown but to a breakthrough, to a new order of mankind." I need sensitivity to that in my own life and in the lives of my children. Listen to this letter Ed Dayton wrote to his oldest daughter as it appeared in the MARC *Newsletter* by World Vision. In it I sense one generation catching a glimpse of God's call to another:

> We used to say when she was a little girl that she was born old. I suppose that was because she was our first and the other two came so close. We just expected that a

three-year-old was her mother's helper in caring for the others. But she was like that. Not that she was always serious. No one could come up with more imaginative ways to have fun. It was more the questions she asked, questions that sounded as though perhaps they could have waited for another five years. She grew up so fast. A girl particularly sensitized to the world around her. A helping girl.

She had a way of understanding things on the basis of very little input. Her roommates in college were continually distracted by the way she could scan a textbook the day before the exam and draw out of that brief encounter not only enough to pass, but that which seemed to synthesize what she had read into an A+.

But there are penalties for being serious about life. The more we understand about the world, the more tragic a place it appears and the more impossible to change. Near the end of college it all seemed to catch up with our Jill. It no longer seemed worth the effort. Pressures of personal relationships and a troubled engagement seemed to close in and at times almost overwhelmed her. Somehow the beautiful future kept eluding her grasp. It was as if a dark cloud was always in the corner of every picture she painted. But college ended. She came back and for a year worked as a secretary. That required very little training. So her energies moved in other directions. Her deep understanding of God's Word and how it applied to single young women drew around her a group who found in her a strength beyond themselves and beyond her too.

How unexpected at times are God's leadings. . . . Two months after she planned a trip to Africa with me she met a missionary in Northern Kenya. Six months later, one week before we left for Europe and Africa, she told her mother that she loved the young man and believed God wanted her to marry him.

And now they are on their way to Kenya. It's a hot, dry, dusty place. They serve a nomadic tribe whose culture in many ways is offensive to any Westerner. There aren't many people like her there. I guess there aren't many people like her in the world! I wish I could go with her, just to be there to keep telling her, "It's all right. It's all right." God knows all about those dark clouds. Yes, He does ask us to sacrifice, but there is always more joy that comes bursting through the thunderheads as though those clouds were really just symbols of His glory, like the cloud He used to lead His people three thousand years ago.

Oh, Jill! Life is such a special adventure. And God has blessed you and Ray so richly with so many things. Take that overflowing cup to that dry, thirsty land and pour it out abundantly. And every evening you'll discover there is some left for you.

11 { *The Beautiful People*

The beautiful people—Who are they? "The midnight jet to San Francisco just for the party. Seats on the fifty-yard line for every single Rams' game at home or away." So runs the ad. And the young girl in it says, "Long slinky dresses or old ratty levis. Bacon and eggs at dawn before I go to bed. In favor of honesty between men and women. Friends with men I used to be in love with."

Is that what it takes to make life beautiful? If it is, why keep on with the hassle of trying to get everybody dressed and moving to church on Sunday? Even when we make it who can leave at home all the feelings and problems we live with during the week? So there we sit, edgy wives, preoccupied husbands, uncertain and yet very sure young people. And often as I leave I feel like Emerson who once said, "Went to church today and came home not feeling overly depressed."

Where can I get my hands on a style and quality that makes life beautiful? Suddenly I remember something David did at the height of his career, something beautiful. It stands out like a green oasis in a desert of rock and sand. I watch him sitting quietly by himself lost in thought. So

many people reach their conclusions about life like grade
school children. They cheat by copying the answers out
of a book without working the problem out for themselves. David took time out to let eternity in. His mind
goes back over those days when he had gone hungry and
lived like a hunted animal out in the caves and rocks hiding
from Saul. The thought of Saul's hatred still makes his
blood run cold.

Then suddenly he asks out loud, "Is any member of
Saul's family left alive to whom I could show kindness for
Jonathan's sake?" What a beautiful idea! No hint of an
ememies list. Rather David wonders if he had an enemy
left that he could help. He soon found out that years
earlier when news of the Israelis tragic defeat under Saul
at Mount Gilboa reached the capital, a nurse grabbed up
Jonathan's small son, Mephibosheth, and ran for their lives.
In her panic she dropped the boy. For the rest of his life
he hobbled along on crippled feet.

It's strange how innocent children so often bear the
scars of someone else's human failure. I see so many young
people growing up with twisted scarred personalities because of unthinking or unfeeling friends or parents or
teachers. Nor can I shake from my mind the pictures of
Vietnamese children suffering the cruelties of war.

We live interdependent lives. On a broad scale the
energy crisis underscores that fact. I know some people
suggest the fantasy of economic self-sufficiency for the
United States in an effort to get our country moving in
research and development of new energy resources. But
even if we could become self-sufficient in our energy resources, many of our allies and friends cannot. And with
the emergence of the Arabs with their vast increasing cur-

rency reserves as well as energy reserves, I get the feeling that a major shift in economic and political power has occurred. I do live in an interdependent world. I see that in such a world I suffer for the sins of others just as surely as the sacrifice of others saves me.

In any case, Mephibosheth, as Jonathan's son, became heir to Jonathan's throne. But David sat on that throne. And I know how often political leaders, once in power, tend to see their rivals as enemies. Mephibosheth knew it too. So he took pains to steer clear of David. He kept a low profile in the back country of Lo-debar. The word *Lo-debar* means "barren land." A place of frustration and emptiness. That's where Mephibosheth lived. And that's how he lived. He lived a barren, frustrated, empty, bitter life. "Why should God let this happen to me? If he's God, why doesn't he do something to straighten things out? I should sit on the throne, not David."

And suddenly in an era fraught with bitterness and resentment David did a beautiful thing. The memory of his friend, Jonathan, still brought out the best in him. He knew he had to do something to unite his people. Of course he could have stuck to working out programs to match each new crisis in a kind of detached impersonal way. But David knew justice meant caring about people. If a man needs help, why not help him regardless of his particular ideology or point of view? And David had the sense to see that national health depended upon the health of all the people—even Saul's family, his political "enemies." He probably thought to himself, "Is there any member of Saul's family left to whom I can show kindness for Jonathan's sake? Anyone to whom I may show the kindness God requires?"

The kindness that God requires—what's that? Well, it's a way of living life that often goes against my inclinations, my own self-interests, my own cultural conditioning, to want to do something right. That's what the kindness that God requires means. And usually the influence of a great friend brings that out in me. I receive that kind of grace every day of my life. Without it I'd have trouble living a moral life at all. Wherever I find the power of healing, recuperation, renewal at work, I see the kindness of God.

I don't think any person on earth, good or bad, can escape that gracious influence. Nor does God attach any strings to his kindness. It does not depend on a person's behavior. It's not a matter of "I'm acceptable to God, if. . . . " I often behave badly, and when I do, I feel unworthy of the trust others have in me. Yet despite the kindness of God I often have trouble showing kindness to other people. Worse yet, I'm often not even kind to myself. For one thing it saves me a lot of trouble. Yet in the process I lose a lot of friends and miss a lot of fun.

One Saturday I sat out in our back yard between rain squalls talking to our youngest son, Gary. "I like it out here," he said, "it feels like we're up in the mountains." We got to talking about our experiences in the mountains. As we talked the sun suddenly came out from behind the clouds. I could feel warmth on my arms and on my forehead. And suddenly I remembered how Jesus said, "God makes his sun rise on good and bad alike, and sends the rain on the honest and the dishonest" (Matt. 5:45). The sun shines regardless of my behavior. God's kindness does not depend on my goodness. He's not interested in seeing that I get all I deserve. He's concerned to see that I get what I need! That's the beauty of it. That's the kindness that saves.

David understood this. And suddenly I see the Spirit of God loose in his life. David saw what his nation required. It would take a great kindness to bring the healing that would make his country whole again. So he decided to act as graciously as he could to a member of Saul's family. Mephibosheth could never buy that kindness. It came as a gift. That's the beauty of it and the beauty of people who have that style.

No wonder Jesus shocked so many. He simply threw away the idea that by good behavior people could somehow deserve the kindness of God. In a scandalous way he welcomed unclean, undesirable, disrespectful people the minute they showed any interest in him. People had always had it in the back of their heads that a person had to qualify for God's approval. And here came Jesus showing kindness to all kinds of unqualified people who felt guilty and embarrassed. And he did it all in God's name. It just didn't seem fair. But it was so beautiful. No one had seen anything quite like it before.

Jesus kept pointing out that God doesn't waste time adding and substracting points for my good or bad behavior. He said none of us measure up to the person we could or should be. Inspite of that fact, God sends his kindness to all of us. And he keeps on doing it in this world where I hear so much complaining from people about how badly they are treated.

And I understand how a person can get angry at God because he is kind to the unthankful and the evil. I believe he should show kindness to a deserving person like me. Show kindness to undeserving people—how could he?

David and Jesus saw things correctly. It seemed to them that God had declared an amnesty for every person who ever fell short. And I know what a loaded sound that word *amnesty* has in our day. Yet *amnesty* means "forget it." God simply refused to hold people in legal jeopardy any longer. He refused to prosecute. That kind of attitude is what the cross is all about—what it costs, what it stands for. And the cross alone will save us.

Suddenly I sense some new and profound implications of God's kindness for my personal and our national life. I believe in the kindness of God in general; it's the particulars that hang me up. I find myself saying, "I need the kind of Christianity I can live with. Who can trust a God who goes around showing that kind of kindness to anybody or everybody? It looks beautiful, but it's dangerous. We had better protect God from himself. After all, people should show real repentance before they can expect any kindness. They have to pay their debt. They have to earn their way back into favor."

Suddenly I begin to see why the cross of Jesus scandalized the Jews and the Greeks and the Romans. But to anyone who receives his kindness and understands that is what he expected of them, it is still the power of God for our salvation—our economic salvation, our political salvation.

In that mood David brought Mephibosheth right into his own house and sat him down at his own table. He saw kindness not as an option but as an essential part of a fully human life.

I think David also reflected a profound understanding of political reality. Mephibosheth now sat right next to him at dinner. What a beautiful way to make an ally out of a rival by letting him receive your kindness every day!

What better way to hinder his working behind your back than to keep him where you can see him?

David showed not only his understanding of God but his political savvy. That's the beauty of this man. He had a clear, cool head to give his warm, kind feelings direction. Kindness never means rash trust of anybody. I have seen how gracious intentions often flop because the person who offered them did not get his head in gear. That hurts everybody and makes a second effort doubly hard.

So Mephibosheth sat down at David's table. He had plenty to eat, freedom from want. As long as he sat at that table, he did not have to fear an assassin's dagger. And David gave him back all the property of his grandfather, Saul. In other words he opened up the door of economic power to him. That's the beauty of God in human nature.

And this example should open my eyes. What is it that the repressed people in Korea, Brazil, Spain, Russia, or Africa want? Isn't it what Mephibosheth needed—freedom from want, freedom from fear, freedom to say what he wanted, an access into the economic realities and power of the world? No matter how unattractive some people may look to me, how much their demands may shock me, how warped, embittered, twisted by pain or shame such people seem to me, they need what Mephibosheth needed! They need a strong friend able to forget past grievances who can demonstrate in a clearheaded way the kindness so characteristic of the living God who loved us and gave himself for us in Jesus Christ. And I am in a beautiful position to begin to think and to live like that before I die.

12 *A Crisis of Moral Relaxation*

But suddenly, without warning, the beauty can drop out of life. I start feeling haggard and ugly. Why? Honest men differ in their analysis of the situation. Unfortunately in a crisis of any kind, honesty is never enough.

For instance, one man honestly believes the government must do more. Another man just as honestly believes the government has already done too much. Honesty isn't the issue. Moral judgment becomes critical. The real frontier before us today lies in the field of moral judgment.

Why, some years ago, did world opinion from London to New Delhi react so violently to the American use of napalm in Viet Nam? At that time our Secretary of State tried to stem the tide of opinion by asking why no one raised similar protests against atrocities committed by the Viet Cong and the Vietnamese. One answer, not the only one of course, is that the Western world professes to live under the God and Father of our Lord Jesus Christ; the Eastern World does not.

Why raise that issue? Because the values we profess

make us terribly vulnerable. If the communists, whose value system admits no such ethical restraints, practice atrocities, they do commit savagery. But I cannot accuse them of hypocrisy.

If I profess different values, that puts me in a different position. If I condone savagery, I add to that cruelty the evil of hypocrisy. So the issue is not simply honesty. The issue is moral judgment. What chaos faulty moral judgment lets loose!

In the Bible I find David at the height of his power and influence. He had worked hard. He had risen as high as a man could rise. Why not relax a little? Now when a border war broke out David sent his chief of staff. He didn't go to the front as he used to. He stayed back in Jerusalem and relaxed. He could take things easy and rest on his laurels.

And then one evening David rose from off his bed and walked upon the roof of the king's house. And from the roof he saw a woman bathing and the woman was beautiful to look upon. David found it only a small step from his new relaxed lifestyle to a little moral relaxation. He saw her, he wanted her, he took her. And that night they conceived an ill-fated child.

Moral relaxation means feeling I can do what I want to do. I can take whatever I want to take and am strong enough to take. David had that style about him now. If he saw a piece of property, he took it. If he saw a city, he took it. Now he saw a woman, and he took her.

His actions were perfectly legal. The laws of the day permitted more than one wife. David already had several. Yes, this woman had a husband, but a king could legally take what he wanted. Other kings had done so. And David wanted her. Why couldn't he have her? He did have her.

But he made a mistake. Technically he committed no crime. It's just that in his middle years he took a moral vacation from the values he once so highly prized.

I think middle age hits most of us with special force. Middle age snuck up on me. It caught me unaware. I had quite a time admitting I had entered it.

Those in the middle years carry many of life's heaviest loads. Children do not have to work for a living and grandfather gets only social security and a pension. Who pays the bills? The people in the middle. They pay for the children's education. Their taxes go for old age benefits.

Furthermore, at this point, life has a way of standing up and looking you square in the face. Often it promises nothing new—just more of the same. I often get the feeling I've come to a dead end. And I suddenly begin to wonder why I shouldn't just sit back, take it easy, relax.

At age nineteen a lot of us felt we could do so much to make a better world out of the tired, sad arrangement we lived in. But at thirty and beyond a lot of us began to relax and realize how little we could do and how little anything changed. What happened to those idealistic values we started out with? Well, a lot of us just relaxed. But a crisis of moral relaxation brings on a paralysis of values.

And so a depressing number of marriages break up among middle-age people. And a lot of those who stay together do so simply waiting for the children to get old enough to be independent before they call it quits. Do we simply get bored with each other? Or do we feel romance passing us by and that the time has come for a last fling?

A man often feels he has come to a dead end in his profession, he has reached a plateau, he'll go no further. And since he sees little chance of breaking out in that area, he looks for a breakthrough in a personal or sexual relationship.

How vulnerable people become at this age. A lot of us get caught up in a crisis of moral relaxation. What kind of people will we be from here on out? We have to decide.

The decision is a daily choice. Integrity is not like a trust fund set up in my youth that I can sit back and draw on for the rest of my life. Integrity is like a daily wage. It's the result of my daily decisions, my daily sacrifice. And I think what is true personally is true nationally.

So many people I talk to desperately want to be able to trust those who sit in a position of power and responsibility. For awhile a lot of us, according to our point of view, found release for our frustrations in attacking the establishment, rebellious students, permissive education, the military industrial complex, or the media. And then when Watergate broke it dawned on us that lying, cynicism, cheating, arrogance, power grabbing, bribery, and hypocrisy go on at all levels and corrupt all of our institutions.

Suddenly simple words like *good* and *bad*, *right* and *wrong*, *sin* and *salvation*, become decisive again. They rise up out of sociological gobbledygook and political sloganeering which covers over immoral action and explains away every sin. Suddenly I sense I can't have some things without giving up something else. I can't have a strong country and also have poorly paid people, huge corporate profits, group prejudice, class consciousness, elderly sick people uncared for and unthought of. I can't have it both ways. I have to make some moral judgments. That lies at the heart of any moral crisis. What kind of person will I be?

In one episode of the television series "The Odd Couple" Felix and Oscar find themselves for the first time owners of a car. But they can't find a place to park it in New York City. Oscar spends most of his time trying to find a place to park it. Finally in desperation he comes in and announces they will have to sell the car. It takes him a long time to convince Felix.

But then they find they can't sell the car for near its worth. So Oscar says he has an old friend who's a good thief. And he wants to ask the friend to steal the car so they can collect the insurance and get their money out of it. Felix doesn't like the idea. He says something like, "God would never forgive you for such a thing." And Oscar shouts back, "Well, if God owned a car in New York City he would understand."

I cannot trivialize good and bad, right and wrong by trying to smother them with questions like, "Well, what difference does it make," or "Who knows," or "What's in it for me?" When I try that tactic right and wrong turn into a subject for endless debate and religion becomes little more than an ornament. Suppose some things forever displease the Lord. If that's true it may save us from both anarchy and tyranny.

Dr. Karl Menninger in his recent book *Whatever Became of Sin?*, wonders why modern society tries to cope with its moral crisis without mentioning the word *sin*. He feels we need some straight talk which does not equate sin with crime. We don't hear the word *sin* much anymore. Menninger suggests it doesn't mean much. It simply doesn't exist for many people. I seldom hear it except perhaps in a booklet in my hotel room listing the entertainment of the city entitled "Where to Sin in Cincinnati," which gives the word a whole different coloration.

So having dropped the word *sin*, we have only neurotics and criminals. As Menninger says, "No one is responsible, no one is guilty, no one asks any questions, and we all sink into despair and hopelessness." He goes on to point out that successive presidents of both parties have carefully avoided the word *sin* or any call to real repentance. Quoting *Theology Today* he writes, "I cannot imagine a modern president beating his breast in behalf of the nation and saying, 'God be merciful to us sinners,' though experts agree this is one of the best ways to begin. So, as a nation," says Menninger, "we officially ceased sinning about twenty years ago."

But surely the church of Jesus Christ exists in part to call sin, sin, and salvation, salvation. Perhaps you can't determine moral truth by conducting a poll. Let's look further into David's story.

For some time David intuitively felt something had gone wrong. He tried to work it out the way I often try to work out my troubles. He thought he could cover the whole thing up and escape any personal responsibility. He had the whole machinery of government to help him do it.

He called Bethsheba's husband, Uriah, home from the front. Think of the hypocrisy of it! David entertained the man in his palace and got him drunk. He thought, "If I get him drunk he'll go home to his wife and I can blame her pregnancy on her husband."

But the soldier had too much integrity to go home. He

said, "How can I go home and enjoy myself in comfort while my friends are living and dying out in the open fields? I can't do it." So back to the front he went.

And David still had his problem. So he sent word to the general in the field, "See that Uriah gets put in the front rank exposed to the worst dangers of battle." General Joab put him there, and Uriah died.

David took a man's wife, and he took a man's life—all perfectly legal.

I can almost hear David saying to himself, "Why shouldn't I have done it? Can I help the way I'm made? I have powerful sexual needs. I have to satisfy them. Yes, I know I'm the king and should set some kind of standards for the whole country; but everybody else does it. Why shouldn't I? Uriah died fighting for his country. I didn't kill him. An enemy soldier killed him. Legally I'm in the clear."

So David tried to cover the whole thing over. He thought he could hide it from himself and from God. That's where he made his mistake.

Then the Lord sent the prophet Nathan to David's court. And Nathan began to tell a story about a rich man and a lot of sheep and a poor man with one little ewe lamb. The rich man with the great herd takes the poor man's lamb to entertain a guest. The story stabbed David's conscience. "The man who does such a thing deserves to die." And Nathan said, "You are the man." Suddenly David's attempt to hide the terrible naked truth from himself and from his God fell apart.

No man can maintain his self-respect in this world and do things that violate what God has built into creation. I may think I can carry it off for awhile. Then suddenly in the midst of my self-deception I see a cross standing outside the city wall. I watch the best man the world ever saw be killed. My conscience stirs. People who do that sort of thing deserve to die.

And suddenly I hear a voice from beyond the cross, a voice I can't help but recognize as God's, saying, "Art, you are the man! Your indifference, your willingness to tamper with the truth for personal gain, your willingness to play a role to get public approval, your undisciplined desire to get what you want and feel strong enough to take—these things nailed him there."

And my defenses begin to fall apart. I see how I step out of the path of simple truth and justice and mercy. Maturity means calling my sins, sin. I cannot hide them from myself any longer. The light that comes into my darkness hurts my eyes. It pokes into all the nooks and crannies of my desires, my motivations, my secret passions. I don't like feeling exposed like that. And I see why we dropped the word *sin* from our vocabulary.

But whatever became of salvation! Yes, the cross reveals my sin. But it also means my salvation. God does not exist to deplore and condemn. In Christ we face the worst than can happen in a world or in the human heart. My desires may lead me astray. But I need salvation from blindness to my own sins so that by God's grace I can step out into the sweeping vista of hope and healing. Then I can stand a little taller and my troubles seem a little smaller.

Redemption begins to make sense. I can quit cynically saying, "I see no hope and you can't trust anyone anymore." Each day I remember that I live in the light of God's judgment but by the power of his Spirit. Yes, I make some bad moral judgments. But I believe light has come to us in Christ to help us evaluate our moral judgments and give us the will and the power to choose the Way, the Truth and the Life.

13 *The Passing of These Times*

"The times through which he and Israel and all the kingdoms of the world had passed" (1 Chron. 29:30). So the writer brings his story of David to an end. But he sets me to thinking about the times through which I have passed. Yes, "We had joy, we had fun, we had seasons in the sun." But the times often demanded more than I had to give.

I remember the bright lights of the 1939 World's Fair in San Francisco Bay. I could see them from my window. And I remember how suddenly the lights began going out all over the world—dimouts at home, gas rationing, shortages of everything.

But the war ended. I read about the Nuremberg trials and began attending the university, rowing on the varsity crew, falling in love. And I stepped out into the world of the Marshall Plan, the red scare of Senator Joe McCarthy. Then there was Korea, the birth of our children, my first church, the beginning of the Civil Rights Movement, Viet Nam, the assassination of President Kennedy and his brother Robert, and Martin Luther King. And then came Watergate.

What times have passed over us all. Now we struggle to understand and cope with an energy crisis. One man known for his thrift spent several weeks nursing his sick wife. To conserve energy he kept a single candle burning in her room. Suddenly one night she took a turn for the worse. As he left to call the doctor he said to her, "Honey, if you feel yourself sinking, blow out the candle before you go."

Does that sound a little extreme? I mention it because the biblical writers, in speaking of the times through which David passed, mentioned his death in the same breath. I cannot appreciate or understand the times through which I pass unless I come to terms with the end of them. My life contains one absolutely predictable event—someday I will die.

A lot of us still have trouble talking about dying. For years our culture has worked hard to develop a kind of anti-death bias. Dr. Robert Fulton, a Minnesota sociologist, points out that the trend began when the people moved from farms into the city. In cities death gets taken out of our homes and put in hospitals. After World War I we saw the emergence and the increase of funeral parlors and after World War II, the increase of retirement and nursing homes where old people die.

Of course, every child of ten probably has seen ten thousand deaths on television. But in most of these fantasies, the Indian or the yellow man or the black man or the Nazis do the dying somewhere over there. Good Americans seldom die.

But the facts of life keep pressing the questions of death. Old age, as we know it, did not exist prior to this century.

Someone has pointed out that when those now over fifty-five were born, the average man worked seventy hours a week and died at age forty. Now a person works forty hours a week and lives to age seventy.

Like almost everyone else I want to live a long time. But I'm like the Irishman who said, "Sure I want to go to heaven when I die. I know heaven is a grand, wide place. But if someone told me I would be in heaven next week I would take it unkindly!"

I want to live a long time. I do *not* want to grow old and die. Who does? Yet both phrases, "I want to live a long time" and "growing old and dying" mean the same thing. It's just that the phrase "growing old and dying" gets to me. It raises all kinds of uncomfortable questions about poverty or at least substantially less income, maybe chronic illness, or perhaps a nursing home and total dependency. And who wants to experience any of those things?

Listen as Minnie remembers:

God
my hands are old.
I've never said that out loud before
but they are.
I was so proud of them once.
They were soft
like the velvet smoothness of a firm, ripe peach.
Now the softness is like worn-out sheets or
withered leaves.
When did these slender, graceful hands
become gnarled, shrunken claws?
When, God?

They lie here in my lap,
naked reminders of this worn-out body
that has served me too well.

How long has it been since someone touched me?
Twenty years?
Twenty years I've been a widow.
Respected.
Smiled at.
But never touched.
Never held so close that loneliness was
blotted out.

I remember how my Mother used to hold me, God.
When I was hurt in spirit or flesh,
she would gather me close,
stroke my silky hair, and caress
my back with her warm hands.
God, I'm so lonely!

I remember the first boy who ever kissed me.
We were both so new at that!
The taste of young lips and popcorn,
the feeling inside of mysteries to come.

I remember Hank and the babies.
How else can I remember them but together?
Out of the fumbling, awkward attempts of new lovers
came the babies.
And as they grew, so did our love.
And, God, Hank didn't seem to mind if my body
thickened and faded a little.
He still loved it.
And touched it.
And we didn't mind if we were no longer beautiful.
And the children hugged me a lot.
God, I'm lonely!

God, why didn't we raise the kids to be silly and
affectionate as well as dignified and proper?
You see, they do their duty.
They drive up in their fine cars;
they come to my room to pay their respects.
They chatter brightly and reminisce.
But they don't touch me.
They call me "Mom" or "Mother" or "Grandma."

Never Minnie.
My mother called me Minnie.
So did my friends.
Hank called me Minnie, too.
But they're gone.
And so is Minnie.
Only Grandma is here.
And God! She's lonely!
                              —Donna Swanson
                              "Minnie Remembers"

Sure I want to live a long time. It's just that Minnie
reminds me that if I do, I will also grow old, and I will
die. And suddenly I need an understanding that will help
me cope with that as I pass through my times.

Do I really want to go on and on another thirty or
even three hundred or three thousand years with all my
insecurities, with all my loneliness, all my fears, all my
anxieties, simply getting older and older and older? I
doubt it. When someone says, "I don't want to live forever," I know what he means. Who really wants to go on
and on and on, unless—unless once in awhile in these
times through which I pass I dream that life might develop in unimaginable ways?

The man who wrote that ancient biblical story com-
bines the times through which David passed with his

death. What times! He was a shepherd boy who tuned his harp to God and sang, "The Lord is my shepherd, I shall not want"; a teenager who walked through the ranks of dispirited demoralized people out into the valley of decision, and Goliath fell. Then he became an outlaw with a rag-tag collection of cutthroats hiding in caves from the authorities and a jealous King Saul. Finally, he was king himself and builder of the capital at Jerusalem. Then came his seduction of Bathsheba and his attempts to cover it up which led to the rebellion of Absalom and continued civil strife to the end of his days. Yes, he repented and received forgiveness. But those final days of reaping what he had sown went on. Through such times David passed.

To what end had David invested his life? Or did he simply spend it? Worse yet, had others spent it for him? I remember reading of a Presbyterian minister who hadn't missed a Presbytery meeting in forty-two years. Undoubtedly that's a record of some kind. But I couldn't help wondering, "Dear God, had he ever learned how to invest his own life or did other people simply spend his time for him?" So I recently sat in a committee meeting taking stock of myself and wondering about how often I have been compelled to give hours of thought and enormous energy to a lot of things I could very well do without.

And here's something else I've noticed about the times through which I have passed. Have you ever taken out an old photograph album and looked at pictures of how you dressed twenty years ago? When I do, I wonder how in the world I wore such stuff. But the eyes of twenty years ago saw those clothes as beautiful. I wouldn't have worn anything else. But the eyes of today looking at those same clothes laugh or say they look pitiful beyond words.

The same thing happens to ideas. No matter how my views change I usually feel that the ideas, the point of view I have right now is the right one. At last I see clearly. Today I know the truth. But I know that my children twenty years from now will probably wonder how in the world poor old Dad could have believed or thought such things.

I pass through such times. And I need some understanding of my place in them and the significance of my life and the end to which I'm moving. I need to understand what all this means for Art Sueltz and what it means for Art Sueltz to die.

In the New Testament I read, "I wish you not to remain in ignorance, brothers, about those who sleep in death: you should not grieve like the rest of men, who have no hope. We believe that Jesus died and rose again; so it will be for those who died as Christians; God will bring them to life with Jesus" (1 Thess. 4:13–14).

Nothing has blurred my understanding of eternal life more than the idea that it simply means an endless extension of time that goes on forever and ever with little to do but sing hymns. That leaves a lot of us out because we don't have the voice for it and we find the hymns difficult now. Someone once wrote,

I'll be where loud anthems is always ringing.
But as I've no voice, I'm clear of the singing.
Don't mourn for me now, don't mourn for me never.
I'm going to do nothing for ever and ever.

But who needs that kind of existence? And who wants

to wander around forever as some sort of ghost? Suddenly I sense Paul isn't talking about some kind of disembodied spirit that simply goes on and on and on no matter what happens. In fact I don't find that idea anywhere in the Bible. Jesus died. Every last bit of him. And so do I. We believe Jesus died and rose again and the rest of us who die, God will bring to life with Jesus.

I need to know what that statement means. Surely it means at least that in the darkness and the dying those events do not have the last word about my life.

But I will not go on and on as some disembodied spirit. People noticed a qualitative difference about Jesus when they saw him Easter morning. No ghost floated into the room. Yes, they noticed a difference but they noticed he was also the same. He ate with them—not just once but several times. And he said, "Touch me, I'm not a ghost or an apparition."

And all of that experience in Jesus' life affects my understanding of my dying. Maybe you can remember the last dream you had. Any dream will do. I have had one off and on for the last couple of years. As near as I can remember it I'm in a large city. Somehow I'm standing near the front of an unfamiliar, huge, old gothic cathedral full of dark consecrated lumber. It must seat two thousand people. It's empty except for two or three people who stand talking to me.

Suddenly I'm aware that I'm pastor of this great empty cathedral. I start feeling very anxious, so I walk outside and find myself standing, not in a strange city, but in the church yard of our old church in Hanford, California. The manse that burned down fifteen years ago still stands. It's late evening. The lights come on. But the strangers have turned into my wife. However, I can't find my children anywhere. I don't know where Steve, Fay and Garret are. Summer has ended. I don't understand that either. But everyone is leaving town.

I start talking to my wife Millie trying to figure out what has happened to us. Why did we leave Long Beach? Why do I feel like the bottom has dropped out of everything? I feel like I'm dying.

Suddenly I wake up. What a relief! I know where the children are. I'm not in a strange city. I'm not pastor of some vacant cathedral. I'm not even back in Hanford. I'm alive. I'm hopeful. I'm not anxious and depressed. And I don't feel like dying. None of those things that supposedly happened happened at all. It was a dream.

Now for just a minute turn the picture around. Try to imagine that I hadn't dreamed all that. That all of it actually happened. And then suppose that at the moment I felt the bottom dropping out of everything and I felt like I was dying that I wake up. And suppose dying is like waking up! Waking up from a dream that has terrorized and threatened us too long. Then how would I feel?

Of course I don't know for sure, but I have an idea that my sensations a few minutes after I die will be something like the sensations I now feel when I wake up from a troubling dream.

I suddenly wake up not to a strange life, but to a life gloriously familiar. I feel at home. What a relief when I recognize that the experiences leading up to my death were something like the experiences of a dream. While I was in the dream I didn't question anything. People changed a dozen times. Strangers turn into my wife and then they turn into old friends and then they turn into strangers again. That doesn't seem at all strange to me when I dream. But then I wake up. And I'm beginning to sense that the experience of death will feel something like that. I will wake up to new relationships where life stretches out all around me in ways I hadn't thought possible before.

And I have a feeling the only thing I will miss are the friends who seemed alive when I died. Friends I left behind. But then I probably won't expect to see them because they're still sleeping! A perfectly natural and wholesome condition. It's just that I woke up before they did. But I'll know they'll wake up pretty soon. And I won't feel any more separated from them than I feel separated from my son, Gary, when he's taking a nap in the bedroom.

Just one other thing. Once in awhile when I'm dreaming, I know it. I know I'm dreaming. And that does something to the anxiety I feel when I'm dreaming. Those moments in a dream when I know I'm dreaming take the fear out of it.

Which simply means that now and again during this life I come to moments where I feel keenly aware of a qualitatively different kind of life for which I'm built— life liberated from the confines of time and liberated to infinite possibilities of growth and fulfillment. What relief those moments bring to the times through which I pass. In such moments I see clearly that joy and peace and wisdom and honesty and love and understanding are the basic facts of life. In such moments I sense I'm called to to that kind of life and can begin to live it now.

So when I'm anxious and feel like the bottom has dropped out, I know I'm not moving toward a dead end. I should not grieve like other people who have no hope.

Yes, I will die. I believe Jesus died. But I also believe that he rose again. And I believe so it will be with those who die in Christ. God will bring them to life with Jesus.

Someone patient and kind waits for me to wake up. And that understanding of my dying helps me pass through these times. It helps me know that love, integrity, joy, peace, health, wisdom, and clear-eyed vision are real and all the rest is passing away.

Study Guide

I've prepared this study guide to help you relate to what I've written. You can use it by yourself or with a group of people. I've told you what I've seen and what that leads me to believe. Look back over it. Now what do you think? Do you see any spiritual resources that may help you through the passages of life?

If you can talk over what you see with a group of friends I think you'll see even more—and have more fun. So I've designed this study guide for personal reflection that can lead to group interaction. Of course someone needs to lead a group. You can do it, or you can pass the leadership around among your friends in the group.

Before the group meets ask everybody to read the chapter you plan to talk about. Make a few notes as you read. Then look over the questions which follow. They should help you get a good discussion going. If you think of better questions, use them. As the discussion develops, allow people to express themselves without fear of criticism. An atmosphere of acceptance gives people a chance to change and grow. But try to keep the conversation on the track without stopping the flow. Good luck and God bless you.

Chapter 1: *Summertime*

1. Chapter 1 suggests that chaotic forces exist in the hearts of most people in the world. Do you feel such forces at work within you? Do you see them in your community? Your church? Make a note of what you feel and see.

2. Genesis 1 speaks of primeval forces of chaos. But what difference does that make? What possible application could it have to your life? How, if at all, does it help you understand the presence of God in creation today?

FOR DISCUSSION

3. If you are meeting as a group for the first time have everyone introduce themselves. You might do this by asking each person to introduce themselves by answering a question like: "If I could live anywhere in the world with all expenses paid I would live in. . . ." Then decide among yourselves how often you will meet and who will lead your discussions.

4. Now look at question number one above. Do you feel any chaotic forces at work in yourself? Share your notes on what you feel. Do you agree with the statement of Sir Thomas More, that "When men surrender their private conscience to achieve public ends they lead people on a short road to chaos"?

5. In what sense do you think a person's inner turmoil might be the movement of the Spirit of God in that person's

life? Does God have anything to do with our feelings of dissatisfaction? Can you think of any evidence for or against such an idea from your readings in the Bible?

6. Do you agree with the statement, "Christ saw dangerous chaotic events filled with the promises of God"?

Chapter 2: *It All Depends On Your Point of View*

1. This chapter suggests that to live in this world we must continually develop new ways of seeing things. What do you think about that idea? What kind of changes might occur in a person's life because of a change in the angle of his inner vision? Write down what you think such changes might be.
2. 1 Samuel 17:1–58 tells the story of David's conquest of Goliath. What does it say about how he saw that situation in contrast to the other Israeli soldiers? His brothers? King Saul? Goliath? Does it say anything about your perception of current events?

FOR DISCUSSION
3. Do you find yourself today in a situation where your point of view differs substantially from that of your family? Your boss? What useful techniques have you discovered to cope with such conflicts?
4. Do you think God ever takes sides? Or do you think God remains neutral on the issues of personal and community life? Can you ever know for sure which side God takes?
5. Can you describe a situation in which you felt terribly threatened and yet found yourself doing something unusual, something you would not ordinarily do? How do you feel about the statement, "Circumstances don't defeat people,

their inner perceptions do. Opportunities exist even in threatening events, if I could just see them." I have told you of my ambivalence in trying to live out my faith in God. "How easy to love him in the abstract, how difficult in the concrete." Does that check out with your experience? In what way?

6. If you think, in spite of any ambivalence you might feel in your faith, that God loves you and thinks highly of you, what evidence do you have for that? In what ways might that help you see the world differently?

Chapter 3: *Conflict*

1. Many people find *conflict* a frightening word. They find it hard to believe in the positive possibilities that come only through struggle. What shall we do when conflict arises? How can we minimize the damage and maximize the benefits?

2. This chapter uses 1 Samuel 18:1–16 as an example of human conflict. Where do you find yourself most often in conflict with other people?

FOR DISCUSSION

3. How do you feel about the statement, "The argument isn't as important as the way you fight and resolve or do not resolve the conflict"? Do you feel that sooner or later conflict can only be resolved by becoming personal? We can debate theories for ever and ever and never come together. Think of the last personal conflict you had and ask yourself the question, "What is it *in me* that causes me to respond to this person or idea in this way?" Make a note of your response. If you feel comfortable, share it with others in the group.

4. Do you think we can move to a place of healing and

reconciliation even though we may not agree ideologically? What would such a resolution require? What part do trust and honesty play in the resolution of conflict?

5. In the resolution of conflicts what percentage of time do you think should be spent in dealing with feelings rather than the issue itself? Do you find anything in your religious experience that might help you to welcome conflict and use it redemptively?

Chapter 4: *When You Need a Friend*

1. Henry Ford once wrote: "Your best friend is he who helps to bring out of you the best that is in you." Can you think of one true friend outside the circle of your immediate family? Make a note if you can of how this person gave your life a lift.

2. 1 Samuel 18, 19 and 20 tell us of the great friendship of Jonathan and David. Do you think these chapters over-emphasize the importance of human friendship? If not, what bearing does this story have on human relations today?

FOR DISCUSSION

3. Find a piece of paper and sit down in a quiet place and write down every single quality that you would like in a friend of yours. If you feel free, share your list with others in the group. Do you see anything hindering you from becoming the kind of friend you would like to meet?

4. A Chilean writer once wrote of "tavern friendships"—friendships based on conviviality or mutual entertainment. And Frederick Nietzche coined the term "star friendship"—friendships of convenience for people who have very little in common, a kind of detente. How do you feel about the

statement, "Few people have the courage to mature unless someone believes in them"? Have you ever felt that someone loved you deeply and boldly? What were the implications of that love?

5. In what sense if any do you think the words of Jesus, "I no longer call you servants, I call you friends," apply to you today? When if ever can you remember first thinking of God as your friend? What evidence did you have for thinking that?

Chapter 5: *The Original Love/Hate Relationship*

1. I cannot read the Bible without soon realizing that part of the power of God's people comes from the clear recognition they were by no means popular or generally accepted. Hostility need not take us by surprise. Sometimes it comes from within our families, sometimes from our best friends, and sometimes from those for whom we have gone out on a limb. What spiritual resources have you discovered for coping with hostility?

2. Read 1 Samuel 24 as though you had never heard the story before. Forgetting for a minute what you've heard preachers or teachers say about this story, what would you think if you had heard it for the first time?

FOR DISCUSSION

3. Can you remember a time when someone you didn't particularly like treated you graciously? If you can, how would you describe what went on inside of you as a result? Did anything change in your relationship with this person? Did any changes go on inside of you? Make a note of these and if you feel free, share them with the group.

4. In the whole matter of loving "enemies" do you see any difference in being open and gracious, and being emotionally suicidal? Do you think people need to put together their own emotional and spiritual "survival kit" in order to follow Christ in this regard? If you do, what would your kit consist of? Jot down the items you would include.

5. Now suppose for a minute you do something you feel important and right but your behavior does not match the expectation of significant people in your life. How do you feel when you discover their attitude? More importantly, what do you do? How do you try to maintain your integrity and their friendship? How far do you go in either direction?

Chapter 6:   *Remember Who You Are*

1. Please read the first five paragraphs of this chapter again. To what extent does this describe your situation? Take about five or ten minutes to write out your definition of the word *soul*.

2. According to this chapter, Abigail had some advice she felt David needed to hear. What do you think about the advisability of giving unasked for advice? How do you feel when people give you unasked for advice, for your own good, of course?

FOR DISCUSSION

3. If you are with a group take a few minutes to compare and contrast your definitions of the word *soul*.

4. Do you ever ask for someone else's advice or opinion about how you do your job and how you might do it better? Elizabeth O'Connor in her book *Our Many Selves* comments, "Many of us will find that one word of criticism cancels out

ten of praise. We hear criticism as a representative of the person's total response to our total person rather than as a comment on one aspect of our multifaceted self." How do you feel about that statement? Do you listen when people criticize you? Do you grow angry? Do you try to justify yourself?

5. I find that many of the finest people I know see little connection between their job routine and their religion. And I have friends who retired early to give time to things that really interested them. But many of us cannot retire early. And many of us because of limited skills cannot change jobs. We have house payments to make, and our families might starve. Besides, my work-connected stress could follow me into another job. If money were no object and you knew you could not fail, how would you solve such a dilemma? Make notes on your solution. And then if you meet as a group, share your notes.

Chapter 7: *Down But Not Out*

1. I've had parents say, "Won't it be great when the children are grown and on their own?" But when that day actually came, these people felt terribly depressed. What kind of outside pressures bring on depression of spirits in you? In your family? What have you tried to do about them? What things do you especially want to work on?

2. In 1 Samuel 27, David's prayer expresses his feeling about the incompleteness of life. How do you feel about the statement in the chapter, "And it suddenly looks like things will not turn out alright. It feels like no matter how frantically I try I will not build my kingdom before death gets me. The incompleteness of my life tenses me up." Make a note of your feelings.

FOR DISCUSSION

3. How do you feel about the comment, "A rundown body invites a rundown spirit. A chemical imbalance can put me into an emotional powerdive"? How much ordinary depression do you feel comes as a psychological fallout from poor health habits? What changes, if any, would such an understanding make in your pattern of life?

4. How much truth do you see in the statement, "People don't change because someone tells them to. They change as someone listens"? Try to think of someone outside of your immediate family whom you first remember listening to you. Who was this person? What did they do? What happened to you as a result of feeling that someone heard you? Can you remember the first time you spent an hour listening to someone tell you their tale of woe? Do you need to hear the same story over and over from the same person? At what point have you heard enough?

5. How do you feel about life's "deadends"? In what sense, if any, does your experience check out with that of the New Testament writer who heard the Lord saying, "Behold I make all things new"?

Chapter 8:   *When Things Fall Apart*

1. Millions of people all over the world seem to realize suddenly that they cannot live by science or affluence alone. Meaning for our existence does not arise out of matter. Unless something comes to us from beyond what is visible, the visible world remains meaningless. But "Is that enough to face life with? Just God?" Think about this for a minute and make a note of your reactions.

2. Read the scripture passage 1 Samuel 29 and 30:1-7 in a modern translation such as the New English Bible. In what

sense if any can you find parallels between this story and your own experience. What relevance does it have for society in general today?

FOR DISCUSSION

3. With so many national and international social problems pressing for immediate solution, to talk about personal experience may seem individualistic and socially naïve. Yet even a brief reading of history indicates that every generation seems to have a central, pervasive, human dilemma around which gather the more obvious external social and institutional crises. Suppose God can speak specifically to each generation's dilemma in a way that common people can understand. Can you think of a time when you felt close to God? Can you describe it? When did it happen? Where did it happen? How did it happen? Can you remember how you felt as a result? Did your perception of your situation change? What did you do? Make any notes you want and share them with the group if you feel free.

4. William James says that when you buy something the important question to ask the salesman is, "What is your theory of the universe?" It doesn't matter how fine the bargain looks, if the seller has no faith in truth you are smart not to buy from him. What we do and who we are depends so much upon what we believe in. I think you will find it helpful to discuss in a group the question, "What help does Christ give us in making decisions?" Try to be precise and concrete.

Chapter 9: *Out of Patience*

1. This chapter raises an important issue for times when we live at short range looking for quick magical answers. Chris-

topher Morley once described how deeply our "hurry-up" culture can infect us.

> I who all my life had hurried
> Came to Peter's crowded gate,
> And as usual was worried
> Fearing that I might be late.
> So when I began to jostle
> (I forgot I was dead),
> "Patience," smiled the old apostle,
> "Take your eternity," he said.

At what points in life do you feel the greatest impatience? Do you feel satisfied that you get impatient about the right kinds of things? How could you change?
2. As you reread 2 Samuel 5:1–5 do you sense anything about David's attitude over his wait at Hebron?

FOR DISCUSSION
3. Discuss your reaction to the following quotations:
  a. ". . . impatience does have virtues. The time comes when you have to quit talking and act. A patient's fever simply does not go down because the doctors discuss his case. The patient could die if they do not act."
  b. "I'm impatient with irresponsibility. I'm impatient with injustice. I'm impatient with imperfection. I'm impatient with myself. Yet while I get impatient with myself and my children I often remain relatively patient with friends and co-workers."
  c. "I know people . . . who get terribly impatient with God. They want quick permanent answers. No more delay. No more nonsense. If impatience works wonders in moving mountains, why not in the development of human nature?"
  d. "Nothing, absolutely nothing in the Bible tells me faith in God will instantly solve my human problems."

e. "But never once does he (God) use his power to drive people to their knees. He keeps waiting and hoping that some of them will see 'the way' and some of them will catch on. I never arrive. And yet I'm always arriving. As Reinhold Niebuhr once commented, 'There was a time when I had all the answers. My real growth began when I discovered the questions to which I had the answers were not the important questions.'"

f. "If God has the patience to allow me to develop, why should I get impatient with myself?"

Chapter 10: *Times of Transition*

1.
Our fathers have been churchmen
For 1900 years or so,
And to every new proposal
They have always answered, "No."

And why not? What a terrible waste of time if every day we had to learn all over how to tie a bow or use a knife and fork! Yet how do you feel about economist Edmund Stillman's statement that we "are thinking ten to fifteen years in the past, laboring under the weight of outmoded ideas that simply do not correspond to present reality"? For example where in the New Testament do you find that we must do the Lord's work in a churchy looking building on the corner at four times on the clock each week: 9:30, 11:00, and 7:30 on Sundays and 7:30 Wednesday night? What are the advantages as well as the disadvantages of custom?

2. How closely do you feel that your ideas of what ought to be done fit with present reality? Can you note three new ideas you have embraced in the last ten years? As you read

2 Samuel chapters 5–7, can you notice any parallels with our contemporary social scene? Make a note of these. Now everything in our universe seems to be on the move. Do you feel that God is "the great exception" to all that movement? Or is he "the chief example" for those positive, forward-moving, good-creating aspects and elements in the world?

FOR DISCUSSION

3.   The text notes that God often says no and he often says no to my highest hopes and fondest dreams. William Faulkner in his novel *The Reivers* comments, "You've got to say goodbye to some things you know in order to say hello to some things you don't." Do you think it's ever possible to claim something new unless or until you willingly outgrow something old? What old ideas could you willingly let go of?

4.   We hear a great deal about appropriate technology today. As the text notes, "suddenly it sounds fashionable to equate a lower standard of living with a less hectic way of life." Yet the country seems closely balanced between the desire for change and reform and the fear that those changes will take something away from the comfortable. In these times of transition do you think change necessarily indicates that what we have done in the past was a failure or was somehow wrong? If not, why not? In what sense, if any, do you think circumstances have altered and now require change? Do we really have the option of choosing the issues which we would like to consider changing?

Chapter 11: *The Beautiful People*

1.   Henry Thoreau has written, "It is something to be able to paint a particular picture or carve a statue, and so to make

a few objects beautiful; but it is far more glorious to carve and paint the very atmosphere in medium through which we look . . . to affect the quality of the day—that is the highest of arts." What better way to affect the quality of your life and others than through acts of kindness. But I have found it more difficult to define kindness than I thought. Take a piece of paper and in twenty-five words or less write your own definition of kindness.

2.   Reread 2 Samuel 9. What correlation, if any, do you find between this story and the following New Testament passages—Luke 6:35, Ephesians 2:7, and Ephesians 4:31–32?

FOR DISCUSSION

3.   If you are meeting in a group, refer to paragraph one and compare your definitions of kindness. What commonality do you discover? What differences? Could you write a joint statement on which all could agree?

4.   You might take a few minutes to quietly review the past forty-eight hours of your life. Can you think of acts of kindness when somebody went beyond the call of duty to help you? In what way, if any do you think God uses such moments to communicate his presence and love for us?

5.   Talk over your reactions to the following quotations from the chapter:

    a.   "I do live in an interdependent world. I see that in such a world I suffer for the sins of others just as surely as the sacrifice of others saves me."

    b.   "If a man needs help, why not help him regardless of his particular ideology or point of view?"

    c.   "God's kindness does not depend on my goodness. He's not interested in seeing that I get all that I deserve. He is concerned to see that I get what I need!"

    d.   "David showed not only his understanding of God but his political savvy. . . . He had a clear, cool head to give his warm, kind feelings direction. Kindness never means rash trust of anybody."

Chapter 12: *A Crisis of Moral Relaxation*

1. According to the late Fred Allen, "A lot of people spend six days sowing wild oats, then go to church on Sunday and pray for a crop failure." In what ways do you feel the values we profess make us vulnerable?
2. As you read the story of David in 2 Samuel 11 and 12, what was your attitude? Were you sympathetic? Repulsed? Tolerant? How would you reconcile this story with Jesus' approach to the women taken in adultery recorded in John 8:1–11?

FOR DISCUSSION
3. Dr. William M. Ramsey once suggested a little quiz you can give yourself to find out what kind of ethics you tend to prefer. Your group might enjoy taking it too. Imagine these situations:

    a. You're tempted to become part of a questionable business deal. What argument would be more likely to stop you:

        (1) The Bible says, "Thou shalt not steal."

        (2) You know that even one dishonest act could easily get you into bigger trouble in the end.

    b. Your marriage is really becoming intolerable. Which kind of consideration would tend to keep you from getting a divorce:

        (1) You promised at the wedding to remain true until death.

(2)   Divorce would probably have a bad effect on your children.

c.   You're trying to decide about whether or not to accept a new job which has been offered you. Which consideration would likely be most influential as you make your decision:

(1)   Your sense of obligation toward your present employer.

(2)   Your salary and fringe benefits of the new job.

4.   How do you feel about the statement in this chapter: "The real frontier before us today lies in the field of moral judgement"? But to make such judgements one must feel convinced he's right. How do you know with conviction what is right? An old maxim runs, "So act that you can will the principle of your act to be universal law." How would you put that old maxim in contemporary language? How do you think you might apply it?

Chapter 13:   *The Passing of These Times*

1.   Psychologist Rollo May wrote, "The confronting of death gives the most positive reality to life itself. It makes the individual existence real, absolute and concrete." In what way, if any, do you think an awareness of your own mortality can help you live a more effective life here and now? Make a note of these.

2.   In the New Testament the Apostle Paul writes in 2 Corinthians 4, "Though our bodies are dying, our inner strength in the Lord is growing every day." Can you think of any evidence from your own experience, or from the lives of people you know, that bears out Paul's testimony?

FOR DISCUSSION

3. Do you think it is ever wise to talk with someone about their dying? Have you ever talked with anyone about your own dying? If not, why not? Can you think of times or situations or persons with whom such conversation would be inappropriate?

4. How do you relate to the statement in the chapter which says, "Who really wants to go on and on and on unless once in a while in these times through which I pass I dream that life might develop in unimaginable ways"? Do you see any way in which the past might give courage for the future? In what ways might the remembering of past joys deepen present reality? Do you think a person ever grows too old to dream dreams and move daily into new areas of adventure? Do you see any difference between novelty and newness?